Crazy
for
Scraps

19 favorite quilts from
SALLY SCHNEIDER

Martingale®
& COMPANY

Crazy for Scraps: 19 Favorite Quilts
from Sally Schneider
© 2009 by Sally Schneider

That Patchwork Place® is an imprint of
Martingale & Company®.

Martingale & Company
20205 144th Ave. NE
Woodinville, WA 98072-8478 USA
www.martingale-pub.com

Printed in China
14 13 12 11 10 09   8 7 6 5 4 3 2 1

**Library of Congress Cataloging-in-Publication
Data**
Library of Congress Control Number: 2009020310

ISBN: 978-1-56477-926-7

CREDITS

President & CEO ■ Tom Wierzbicki

Editor in Chief ■ Mary V. Green

Managing Editor ■ Tina Cook

Developmental Editor ■ Karen Costello Soltys

Technical Editor ■ Nancy Mahoney

Copy Editor ■ Sheila Chapman Ryan

Design Director ■ Stan Green

Production Manager ■ Regina Girard

Illustrator ■ Laurel Strand

Cover & Text Designer ■ Shelly Garrison

Photographer ■ Brent Kane

MISSION STATEMENT

Dedicated to providing quality products
and service to inspire creativity.

DEDICATION

For Zach, Alec, Dylan, Owen, and George. I love making quilts for you!

ACKNOWLEDGMENTS

Leona VanLeeuwen, for always making time to quilt my quilts, and for doing such a great job on them.

Maureen McGee and Sue Phillips, whose quilts for the original books were so good we wanted to keep them in this one.

Judy Martin, for permission to use the Bard of Avon block from *The Block Book* by Judy Martin (Crosley-Griffith Publishing Co., 1998).

The staff at Martingale & Company, for suggesting a "best of" book. I'm so thrilled to be able to do it.

Nancy Mahoney, for her sensitive editing of my manuscript.

And most of all, the students I've taught, and who have taught me, over the 18 years I've been teaching scrap quilts. Your enthusiasm has encouraged me and your ideas inspired me.

12

18

24

40

44

48

60

64

68

80

84

88

contents

30

36

52

56

72

76

92

6

introduction

I made my first real scrap quilt in 1987 while I was living in Hawaii. I sewed strips together, cut triangles from the strip sets, and then sewed the triangles back together into rows. It was a true disaster. The light fabrics were all in one part of the quilt and the darks all together in another part. There was no rhyme or reason to that quilt, and I ended up donating it to a homeless shelter. But after looking at the finished quilt (and getting over the disappointment of having failed), I wondered what I could do better. It took several more quilts to figure it out, and probably several dozen more to learn the lessons that make better scrap quilts.

I first wrote about scrap quilts in 1990 when That Patchwork Place published my first book, *Scrap Happy*. But more ideas kept popping into my head, so I wrote *ScrapMania* in 1994, then *Scrap Frenzy* in 2001. Imagine my thrill when Martingale & Company recently asked me to do a compilation of those three books. It was like being asked to do a book of "Sally's Greatest Hits"! How exciting is that?

As I reviewed what I wrote in those three books, I realized that my techniques have evolved over the years, especially the way I cut pieces for scrap quilts. I started by using ¾-yard pieces for the scraps (and who wants to dedicate ¾ yard of any fabric to the scrap pile?), but quickly changed that to fat quarters. They were becoming available in abundance, and the beautifully coordinated bundles that I found at quilt shows were almost irresistible—no, they truly *were* irresistible. I realized this the time I came home from a quilt show with 15 bundles of eight fat quarters!

Fat quarters still form the basis of all my scrap quilts. The only extra fabric I purchase is for the background and borders. The fat-quarter packets are the inspiration for color combinations and sometimes even for a whole quilt. Sometimes I let them pile up on my cutting table just so that I can admire the colors and the textures. But eventually they all get cut up and stitched into a quilt.

Although most of my fabric comes from fat quarters, I use other pieces as well. Any time I make a quilt and have fabric left over, I cut it up into specific-sized pieces and add the pieces to the appropriate basket. When quilts come back from the quilter and I trim the edges off, those pieces also get cut up and end up in my scrap baskets. Nothing goes to waste; I can always find a use for those leftover bits. The only thing I don't save is the small cutaway pieces from making folded corners, unless I start with at least a 3½" square. That is a big enough piece to do something fun with.

Two colors that I almost always use in my scrap quilts are red and yellow. I have two reasons for this. First, red and yellow are on the warm side of the color wheel, and we relate to scrap quilts as warm and comforting, so red and yellow accentuate that feeling. The second reason is that my mother said I should! We were talking about gardens at the time, but what she said relates to quilts as well. She told me that every garden needs some red and some yellow flowers to make it sparkle. The more quilts I make, the more I understand how right she was.

Let me inject a bit of caution here; many people think that making scrap quilts will use up their stash of scraps. Nothing could be further from the truth. I don't know how they do it, but my scraps seem to breed, and I usually end up with more than I started with.

strategies for making successful scrap quilts

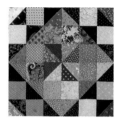

Over the years I've taught quiltmaking, and scrappy quiltmaking in particular, I've met people who are reluctant to make scrap quilts because they are uncomfortable putting fabrics together that don't match or coordinate. But there are ways to make scrappy quilts that are quite comfortable to complete. I have three basic methods of making quilts from all my accumulated fabrics.

First is the coordinated block method. With this method, you make a block from several coordinated prints, but make each block from a different set of prints. Use the same background fabric for the entire quilt and it will all coordinate beautifully (see "Wyoming Valley Star" and "Bard of Avon" at right). Keeping the background constant ties the whole quilt together. I even use the background as the sashing strips in these quilts because it makes the varied blocks float on the background.

The second method I use is a fabric-menu technique. I assign each part of the block a specific color, and then use many fabrics of that color for those parts of the quilt. For example, in the "Blackford's Beauty" quilt on the facing page, all the large star points are red and all the squares are green. But I used many different reds and greens in those positions. Because I had used so many prints for the squares and large stars in that quilt, I chose to make the center small star of each block from the same yellow or gold fabric. There are six different yellow or gold fabrics, one for each block. Again, using just one background fabric, even for the sashing strips, ties all the elements together. Other examples of the fabric-menu technique are "Dawn Stars" and "Fireworks."

Wyoming Valley Star

Bard of Avon

Blackford's Beauty

Dawn Stars

Fireworks

The third method is what I call the brown bag method. When a block is divided into dark and light units, I place all the dark fabrics into a brown bag and the light fabrics into another brown bag. As I sew pieces together, I choose from the bag without worrying if the fabrics look good next to each other. This works particularly well for designs like "Askew" and "Scrap Nine Patch," shown below. When you assemble all the blocks, all you see is the pattern you have created and the myriad of colors you have used. You no longer see individual fabrics.

Askew

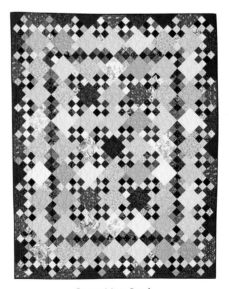

Scrap Nine Patch

VALUE, VARIETY, AND PATTERN

Selecting fabrics is easiest when you understand three important characteristics of scrap quilts—value, variety, and pattern.

value

Value is defined as the relative darkness or lightness of a color. Most quilt patterns are divided into different shapes, and the pattern we see, whether it be a star, a basket, a tree, or some other graphic, is made more obvious by using different values of fabric.

To determine value, you need more than one piece of fabric. That's because value is relative—it depends on what other values are around it. A fabric may be light when you put it with fabric that is darker, but it becomes dark when you put it with fabric that is lighter.

The way I determine the value of my fabrics is to put everything I plan to use in a quilt on the floor, both strips and larger pieces that I may cut into for the quilt. I separate them into piles, one for each value required. Then I look at the piles carefully, checking to see that everything in one pile is a similar value, and that nothing sticks out as being too different. I do this with each pile, checking also that nothing in the dark pile is lighter than anything in the light pile. Squint at the fabrics in the piles to make sure that the values are consistent.

When you are ready to make a block, determine which part of the block should be dark, which part medium, and which part light. Then use a variety of the appropriate-value fabrics to make the block. When you do that, you still get the graphic image, but you can use a lot of fabrics to achieve that image.

variety

I collect all kinds of fabric: floral prints, stripes, plaids, batiks, reproduction prints, novelties, bright and subdued prints, dark and light values, and all the colors of the rainbow (and then some). I use them all, and I often put them all into one scrap quilt. I especially like to use a few novelty or pictorial prints in each scrap quilt; it's fun to see this type of print in old quilts, and I want people to have the same enjoyment when they look at my quilts. My collection includes fabrics depicting bugs, candy bars, wine, junk food, and even sports teams (see "Interweave" on page 60 and see if you can find the Denver Broncos fabric).

But sometimes it's fun to make a quilt from just one type of fabric. I mostly do this with reproduction prints, either Civil War–era or '30s-style prints (see "Perkiomen Valley in the 1930s" on page 76 and "Joseph's Coat" below and on page 64).

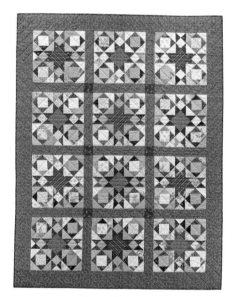

Joseph's Coat

The only fabrics I don't collect and use are solid colors. They seem to become eye-stoppers; because they are so different from prints, your eye tends to stop when it gets to these fabrics instead of going all around the quilt. Of course, all rules are meant to be broken, and Maureen McGee's "Burgoyne Surrounded" on page 30 is ample, and beautiful, evidence of that.

STRATEGIES FOR MAKING SUCCESSFUL SCRAP QUILTS

pattern

The concept of pattern in a scrap quilt is not easily defined. I usually call it a regular repetition of dark and light fabrics throughout the quilt that makes your eye move all around the piece. You don't get stuck somewhere because there are a lot of light or dark fabrics clustered in a particular spot. The diagonal lines in "Interweave," below and on page 60, are the most obvious example—the block itself looks very boring, but when you put several blocks together, the arrangement of lights and darks becomes a dynamic design. While it isn't necessary to use them, traditional patterns are a great source for scrap-quilt designs.

Interweave

CUTTING YOUR FABRICS

All those fat quarters or other pieces of fabric aren't going to do you much good if they aren't easy to use. Can you imagine making a quilt with perhaps 100 fabrics in it? Think of yourself choosing a fabric from your stash, unfolding it, ironing it, trimming the edge, cutting the piece you need, refolding the fabric, then putting it back on the shelf. It would take an awfully long time to just get ready to sew that quilt.

Then imagine if you had a box or basket of fabric pieces already cut to the proper width so that you just had to choose a piece, trim it to size, then sew. You'd be starting on your quilt in much less time, and you'd see it finished even faster. That's the benefit of cutting your fat quarters into strips ahead of time so that they are ready to use.

This is how I cut my strips: from *each* fat quarter, I cut a 1½", 2", 2½", 3", 3½", and 5" strip.

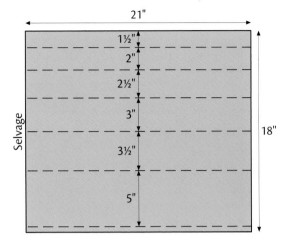

Fat quarter cutting guide

I separate the strips by size and keep them in a wire basket system under my cutting table. Then when I am ready to make a quilt, I just pull out the appropriate wire basket and I'm ready to start sewing. This was a great boon when I wanted to make the "Blackford's Beauty" quilt on page 24. I had a lot of red and green 2½" strips left over from a quilt I made the previous year, and they all worked in my Christmas theme for this quilt. The strips were already cut; all I had to do was cut the pieces to the right size and start sewing. That quilt came together in almost no time at all, just because the cutting was mostly done.

Using these strip sizes is also beneficial because if you have only one strip of a particular fabric, but need more, you can go to the other baskets and find a wider strip of the fabric that you can trim to the size you need.

I must caution you though: it's really easy to fill up the baskets and just keep filling them without making a quilt. My rule of thumb is that when a basket gets full, I have to make a quilt before I can purchase more fat quarters. This often works, but sometimes I just don't want to do that, or the strips in the basket are really old and dated, and I want to work with new fabrics.

When that happens, I have been known to donate a whole basket or two of strips to the ladies at my church who make quilts for the Linus project. Oh, the joy of seeing an empty basket! I get to purchase more fabric, and I get even more excited about making a new quilt.

askew

Finished quilt size: 53½" x 69½" ✳ Finished block size: 4" ✳ Number of blocks: 96

When I was piecing another quilt, instead of using scraps of fabric to start and end the chain-pieced units, I stitched squares and rectangles together to make Mary's Triangle units (see page 101). Thus the Mary's Triangle units in this quilt were bonus units from that other project. I then assembled the units in an asymmetrical arrangement, added a simple appliqué border on a base of scrappy light fabrics, and finished it off with a scrappy red outer border.

MATERIALS

Yardage is based on 42"-wide fabric.

2 yards *total* of assorted dark prints for blocks and appliqués

1¾ yards *total* of assorted light prints for background and inner border

⅞ yard *total* of assorted red prints for outer border

¼ yard of green fabric for appliquéd vine

⅝ yard of black print for binding

3⅝ yards of fabric for backing (2 widths pieced crosswise)

59" x 75" piece of batting

1¼ yards of 16"-wide fusible web

Green and black thread

4½" square of template plastic or Magic Triangle ruler

CUTTING

Cut all strips across the width of fabric (selvage to selvage).

From the assorted light prints, cut a total of:
6 strips, 3½" x 42"; crosscut into 96 rectangles, 2½" x 3½"
14 to 16 rectangles, 7" x varying lengths (from 10" to 15")
4 squares, 7" x 7"

From the assorted dark prints, cut a total of:
7 strips, 4½" x 42"; crosscut into 48 rectangles, 4½" x 5½"
6 strips, 2½" x 42"; crosscut into 96 squares, 2½" x 2½"

From the green fabric, cut:
20 bias strips, 1" wide

From the assorted red prints, cut a total of:
20 to 22 rectangles, 4½" x varying lengths (from 2" to 18")
4 squares, 4½" x 4½"

From the black print, cut:
7 strips, 2¼" x 42"

By Sally Schneider, 2008, Albuquerque, New Mexico.

Quilted by Leona VanLeeuwen.

MAKING THE BLOCKS

Directions are for making one pair of blocks. Repeat to make a total of 96 blocks. After sewing each seam, press the seam allowances in the direction indicated by the arrows.

1. Sew a 2½" dark print square to each 2½" x 3½" light print rectangle. Make two.

Make 2.

2. Sew the units from step 1 together as shown. Clip the seam allowances through the seam line in the center so that you can press the seam allowances away from the dark square, changing the direction of the seam allowance at the center cut.

 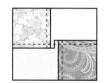

3. Cut the square of template plastic in half diagonally to make a triangle template (or use a Magic Triangle ruler).

4. Pair the unit from step 2 with a 4½" x 5½" dark print rectangle. Refer to "Making Mary's Triangle Units" on page 101 to mark, sew, and cut the blocks. Make a total of 96 blocks.

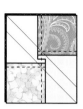 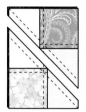

ASSEMBLING THE QUILT TOP

1. Arrange the blocks in 12 rows of eight blocks each. Follow the diagram carefully to correctly position the direction of the large triangles.

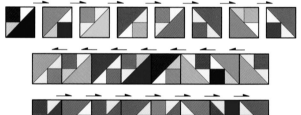

Quilt layout

2. Sew the blocks together in rows, pressing the seam allowances in opposite directions from one row to the next. Then sew the rows together and press the seam allowances in one direction.

3. Measure the length of the quilt top; it should measure 48½". Measure the width of the quilt top; it should measure 32½". Randomly sew the light print 7"-wide rectangles together to make two 48½"-long side-border strips and two border strips 32½" long for the top and bottom borders. Press the seam allowances open. Sew a 7" light print square to each end of the top and bottom borders, pressing the seam allowances toward the border strips.

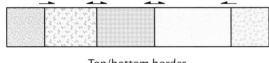

Top/bottom border.
Make 2.

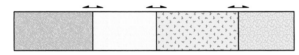

Side border.
Make 2.

4. To make the appliquéd vine, sew the green bias strips together end to end to make one strip approximately 240" long. Fold the strip in half lengthwise, wrong sides together, and press. Open the pressed strip and fold the raw edges to the center; re-press. Cut the long strip into two pieces about 70" long and two pieces about 50" long. Turn one end of each vine under about ¼" and press.

5. Using the photo on page 13 as a guide, arrange the vines on each light print border strip, curving them to your liking. Pin, and then stitch in place using a narrow zigzag stitch and matching thread. Notice that the raw ends of the vines will be tucked under a flower in opposite corners and the finished ends of the vines will be left free.

6. Using the patterns on page 17, trace 12 flowers, 6 hearts, and 15 leaves onto the paper side of fusible web. Following the manufacturer's instructions, fuse the leaves, hearts, and flowers onto assorted dark prints of your liking. Cut out each

shape exactly on the marked line and remove the paper backing. Using the quilt photo as a guide, arrange the shapes on the vines as shown and press them in place. Use black thread to machine blanket stitch around each flower, leaf, and heart shape, leaving a small opening in each corner flower as shown so the vine can be tucked under the flower.

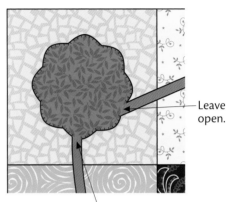

Leave open.

Leave open.

7. Stitch the borders to the quilt, adding the side borders first, and then the top and bottom borders. Press the seam allowances toward the just-added border strips. Complete the appliqué vines, tucking the raw ends under the corner appliqués, and finish machine blanket stitching the flowers.

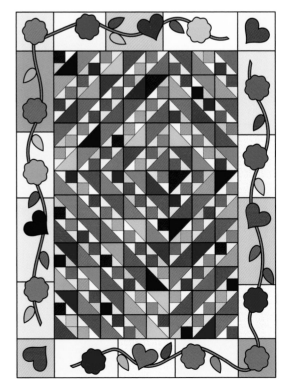

8. Measure the length of the quilt top; it should measure 61½". Measure the width of the quilt top; it should measure 45½". Randomly sew the red print 4½"-wide rectangles together to make two 61½"-long side-border strips and two border strips 45½" long for the top and bottom borders. Press the seam allowances open. Sew a 4½" red print square to each end of the top and bottom borders, pressing the seam allowances toward the border strips.

9. Sew the side borders and then the top and bottom borders to the quilt top, pressing the seam allowances toward the just-added border strips.

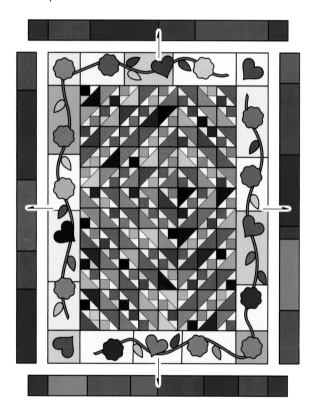

FINISHING THE QUILT

1. Layer the quilt top with backing and batting; baste.

2. Quilt as desired, or follow the quilting suggestion below.

Quilting diagram

3. Referring to "Binding" on page 108, prepare the binding and sew it to the quilt. Add a label.

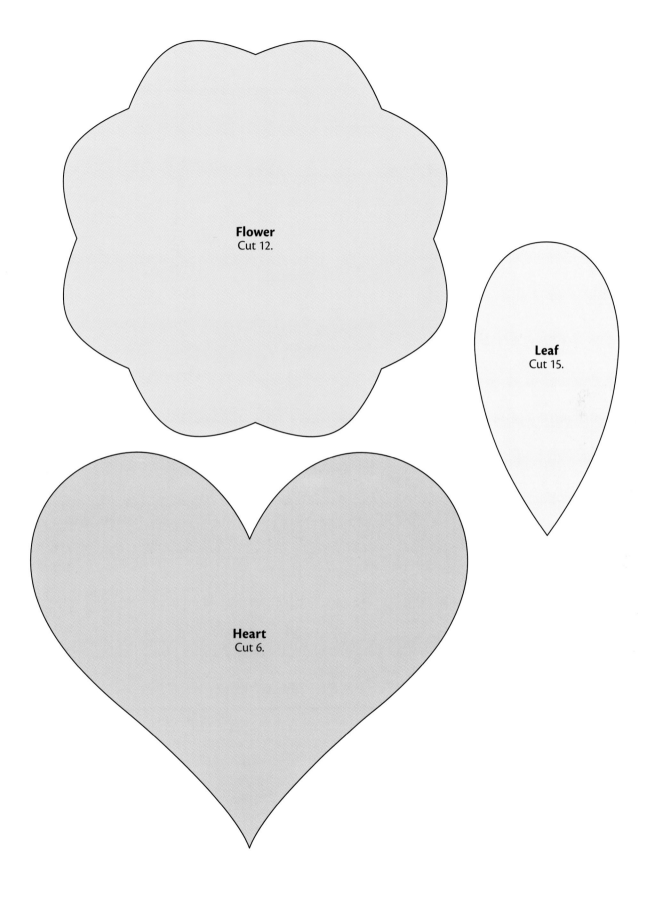

Flower
Cut 12.

Leaf
Cut 15.

Heart
Cut 6.

bard of avon

Finished quilt size: 56" x 76" ✳ Finished block size: 16" ✳ Number of blocks: 6

I chose country-style prints for this design, making it a great comfort quilt. Using the same background fabric for the blocks and the outer border makes the blocks seem to float. The Sawtooth Stars are actually part of the sashing. Block used with permission of Judy Martin.

MATERIALS

Yardage is based on 42"-wide fabric.

3¼ yards of light print for background, sashing, and border

1⅓ yards *total* of assorted dark prints for block and sashing stars

1 yard *total* of assorted medium prints for block and sashing stars

⅞ yard *total* of assorted light prints for block stars

⅝ yard of dark fabric for binding

3¾ yards of fabric for backing (2 widths pieced crosswise)

61" x 81" piece of batting

6½" square of template plastic or Magic Triangle ruler

CUTTING

Cut all strips across the width of fabric (selvage to selvage).

cutting for background, sashing, and border

From the light background print, cut:
3 strips, 16½" x 42"; crosscut into:

    17 strips, 4½" x 16½"

    10 strips, 2½" x 16½"

7 border strips, 4¼" x 42"

3 strips, 3⅜" x 42"; crosscut into 24 rectangles, 3⅜" x 4⅜"

7 strips, 2½" x 42"; crosscut into:

    28 squares, 2½" x 2½" (reserve 4 squares for quilt assembly)

    38 rectangles, 2½" x 4½" (reserve 14 rectangles for sashing)

From the assorted dark prints, cut a total of:
12 strips, 2½" x 21"; from each strip cut 8 squares, 2½" x 2½" (96 total)

12 squares, 4½" x 4½"

Continued on page 20.

18

By Sally Schneider, 2002, Albuquerque, New Mexico.

cutting for blocks and binding

Cutting directions are for one block. For each block, choose 2 dark prints, 1 medium print, and 2 light prints that coordinate.

From dark print 1, cut:
1 strip, 2½" x 21"; crosscut into 8 squares, 2½" x 2½"

From light print 1, cut:
1 strip, 2½" x 42"; crosscut into:

   4 rectangles, 2½" x 4½"

   4 squares, 2½" x 2½"

From the medium print, cut:
1 strip, 4⅞" x 42"; crosscut into:

   4 squares, 4⅞" x 4⅞"; cut each square once diagonally to yield 8 triangles

   1 square, 4½" x 4½"

From dark print 2, cut:
1 strip, 3¾" x 21"; crosscut into:

   2 squares, 3¾" x 3¾"

   2 squares, 2⅞" x 2⅞"

From light print 2, cut:
1 strip, 3¾" x 21"; crosscut into:

   2 squares, 3¾" x 3¾"

   2 squares, 2⅞" x 2⅞"

From the dark fabric for binding, cut:
7 strips, 2¼" x 42"

MAKING THE BLOCKS

Directions are for making one block. Repeat to make a total of six blocks. After sewing each seam, press the seam allowances in the direction indicated by the arrows.

1. Referring to "Making Folded Corners" on page 100, sew a dark print 1 square to one end of a light print 1 rectangle. Trim and press. Sew another dark print 1 square to the opposite end of the rectangle with the seam going in the opposite direction to complete the star point. Trim and press. Make four star-point units.

Make 4.

2. Sew four star-point units, four 2½" light print 1 squares, and one 4½" medium print square together as shown to make the center star.

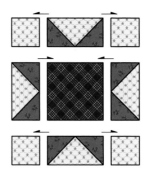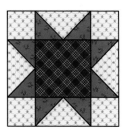

Make 1.

3. Referring to "Method Two" on page 100, place 2⅞" light print 2 and dark print 2 squares right sides together, and then draw a diagonal line from corner to corner on the wrong side of the light square. Sew ¼" from each side of the marked line. Cut the squares apart on the line to create two triangle squares. Repeat with another pair of squares to make a total of four triangle squares.

Make 2 pairs.

4. Sew one triangle square from step 3, one 2½" light background square, and one 2½" x 4½" light background rectangle together to make a corner unit. Make four corner units.

Make 4.

5. Repeat step 3, pairing 3¾" light print 2 squares and dark print 2 squares to make four triangle squares.

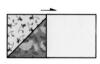

Make 2 pairs.

6. Sew a 3⅜" x 4⅜" light background rectangle to a triangle square from step 5. Repeat with the three remaining triangle squares. Sew pairs of units together as shown. In the center of each unit, clip the seam allowance through the seam line as shown.

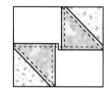

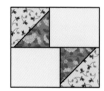

Make 2.

7. Cut the square of template plastic in half diagonally to make a triangle template (or use a Magic Triangle ruler). Align the corner of the template with the pieced unit from step 6 as shown and draw a line along the diagonal edge. Repeat on the opposite corner. Cut on the marked lines to make edge triangles.

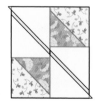
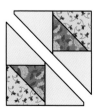

Make 4.

8. Sew two medium print triangles and one edge triangle together to make a side unit. To make matching the pieces easier, with wrong sides together, align the short side of the medium triangle with the long side of the edge triangle. Make four side units.

Make 4.

9. Lay out four corner units, four side units, and one center star from step 2 in a nine-patch arrangement. Sew the units together in rows, and then sew the rows together to complete the block. Make a total of six blocks.

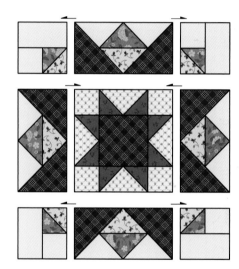

Make 6.

MAKING THE SASHING STRIPS

1. Lay out the blocks and 4½" x 16½" sash-ing strips on a design wall, referring to the quilt layout diagram on page 23 as needed. Arrange the sashing 2½" dark print squares and 4½" dark print squares as desired with the sashing strips, working toward a balanced color arrangement.

2. Using the folded-corner technique, sew a 2½" dark print square on opposite corners of each 4½"-wide sashing strip. Trim and press. Sew a dark print square to each remaining corner of the sashing strip. Make 17.

   You can make each setting star from the same pair of fabrics (one for the center and another for the points), or you can mix up the fabrics.

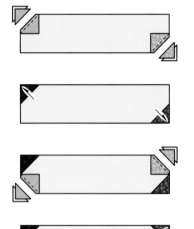

Make 17.

3. Use the folded-corner technique to sew a 2½" dark print square on each end of the reserved 2½" x 4½" light background rectangles to make end pieces for the sashing strips. Trim and press. (These end pieces complete the stars.) Make 14 end pieces.

Make 14.

ASSEMBLING THE QUILT TOP

For detailed instructions, refer to "Quilts with Sashing Strips" on page 104.

1. Return the completed sashing strips and end pieces to your design wall and carefully exam-ine the layout to make sure each piece is placed correctly. Add the 2½"-wide sashing strips and reserved 2½" light background squares as shown in the quilt layout diagram.

2. Sew the blocks and 4½"-wide pieced sashing strips together in rows. Sew a 2½"-wide sash-ing strip to both ends of each row. Make three block rows.

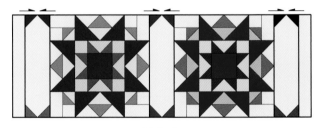

Make 3.

3. Stitch the remaining 4½"-wide pieced sashing strips and the 4½" dark print squares together in rows. Sew an end piece to each end of each row. Make four sashing rows.

Make 4.

4. Stitch two 2½"-wide sashing strips and three end pieces together in rows. Sew a reserved 2½" background square to each end of each row. Make two end rows.

Make 2.

5. Sew the block rows and sashing rows together to form the quilt top, beginning and ending with a sashing row. Sew the end rows to the top and bottom of the quilt top.

Quilt layout

6. Refer to "Borders with Butted Corners" on page 105 to measure, cut, and sew the 4¼"-wide light background outer-border strips to the quilt top. Press all seam allowances toward the outer-border strips.

FINISHING THE QUILT

1. Layer the quilt top with backing and batting; baste.

2. Quilt as desired, or follow the quilting suggestion below.

Quilting diagram

3. Referring to "Binding" on page 108, prepare the binding and sew it to the quilt. Add a label.

blackford's beauty

Finished quilt size: 52½" x 72½" ✳ Finished block size: 16" ✳ Number of blocks: 6

A box of 2½" strips came in very handy when it was time to put this quilt together. All the print pieces started as strips in all the reds and greens that I could find in my stash. I used the fabric-menu technique on page 8 for making this quilt. By dividing the block into sections and assigning a color to each section, but using many prints of each color (except for the small star in the center, which is all the same fabric), I achieved a great scrappy Christmas look.

MATERIALS

Yardage is based on 42"-wide fabric.

2⅞ yards of light print for background and sashing

2 yards *total* of assorted red, green, and gold prints for blocks*

⅞ yard of dark red print for outer border

⅝ yard of dark green for binding

3⅝ yards of fabric for backing (2 widths pieced crosswise)

58" x 78" piece of batting

You'll need at least 6 different gold prints.

CUTTING

Cut all strips across the width of fabric (selvage to selvage).

From the light print, cut:
3 strips, 16½" x 42"; crosscut into 17 sashing strips, 4½" x 16½"

3 strips, 4½" x 42"; crosscut into 6 strips, 4½" x 21"

11 strips, 2½" x 42"; crosscut into:

    12 strips, 2½" x 12"

    36 rectangles, 2½" x 3½"

    48 squares, 2½" x 2½"

From the assorted green prints, cut a total of:
6 strips, 2½" x 21"

6 strips, 2½" x 12"

From the assorted red prints, cut a total of:
48 rectangles, 2½" x 6½"

From *each* of 6 gold prints, cut:
8 squares, 2½" x 2½" (48 total)

2 rectangles, 2½" x 3½" (12 total)

Continued on page 26.

24

By Sally Schneider, 2008, Albuquerque, New Mexico.

Quilted by Leona VanLeeuwen.

From the remaining assorted red, green, and gold prints, cut a total of:
24 rectangles, 2½" x 3½"

From the dark red for outer border, cut:
6 strips, 4½" x 42"

From the dark green for binding, cut:
7 strips, 2¼" x 42"

MAKING THE BLOCKS

Directions are for making one block. Repeat to make a total of six blocks, mixing up the fabrics so you have a variety in each block. After sewing each seam, press the seam allowances in the direction indicated by the arrows.

1. Sew one 2½" x 21" green strip and one 4½" x 21" light print strip together along their long edges to make a strip set. Cut each strip set into eight segments, 2½" wide.

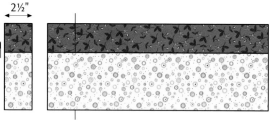

2½"

Cut 8 segments.

2. Sew two 2½" x 12" light print strips and one 2½" x 12" green strip together along their long edges to make a strip set. Cut each strip set into four segments, 2½" wide.

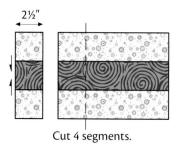

2½"

Cut 4 segments.

3. Sew two segments from step 1 and one segment from step 2 together to complete a corner unit. Make four units.

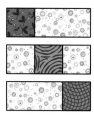

Make 4.

4. Referring to "Making Folded Corners" on page 100, place a 2½" light print square on one end of a 2½" x 6½" red rectangle. Make a total of eight units; sew four with the seams facing in one direction and four with the seams in the opposite direction. Trim and press.

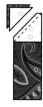

Make 4.   Make 4.

5. In the same manner, sew gold squares on the opposite end of each rectangle from step 4. Be sure to stitch the seams in the same direction as the light print squares.

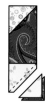

Make 4.   Make 4.

6. Sew the pieced rectangles together, matching the seams. Press the seam allowances open. Make four.

Make 4.

7. Referring to "Method One" on page 99, layer a 2½" x 3½" light print rectangle and a gold rectangle right sides together and draw 45° lines from opposite corners on the wrong side of the background rectangle. Sew on both drawn lines, and then cut the rectangles apart between the lines. Press the seam allowances toward the darker fabric. Make four triangle squares.

Make 4.

8. Lay out four gold triangle squares in a four-patch arrangement. Sew the pieces together in rows, and then sew the rows together to make a pinwheel.

9. Lay out four corner units from step 3, four units from step 6, and one pinwheel in a nine-patch arrangement.

10. Sew the pieces together in rows, and then sew the rows together to complete the block. Make a total of six blocks.

Make 6.

ASSEMBLING THE QUILT TOP

For detailed instructions, refer to "Quilts with Sashing Strips" on page 104.

1. Referring to "Method One" on page 99, layer a 2½" x 3½" light print rectangle and a red, green, or gold print rectangle right sides together, and draw 45° lines from opposite corners on the wrong side of the light print rectangle. Sew on both drawn lines and cut the rectangles apart between the lines. Press the seam allowances toward the darker fabric. Make four matching triangle squares (48 total). Sew four matching triangle squares together to make a pinwheel block. Make 12 blocks.

Make 12.

2. Sew three pinwheel blocks and two 4½"-wide sashing strips together as shown, beginning and ending each row with a pinwheel block. Make four sashing rows.

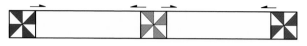

Make 4.

3. Arrange the blocks into three rows of two blocks each. Sew the blocks together in rows with a sashing strip between each block. Sew a sashing strip to both ends of each row.

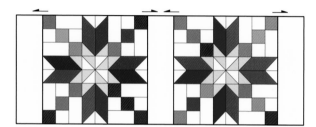

Make 3.

4. Sew the block rows and sashing rows together to form the quilt top, beginning and ending with a sashing row.

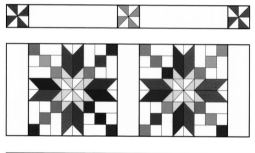

Quilt layout

5. Refer to "Borders with Butted Corners" on page 105 to measure, cut, and sew the 4½"-wide dark red outer-border strips to the quilt top. Press all seam allowances toward the outer-border strips.

FINISHING THE QUILT

1. Layer the quilt top with backing and batting; baste.

2. Quilt as desired, or follow the quilting suggestion on the facing page.

3. Referring to "Binding" on page 108, prepare the binding and sew it to the quilt. Add a label.

Quilting diagram

burgoyne surrounded

Finished quilt size: 85½" x 103½" ✳ Finished block size: 15" ✳ Number of blocks: 20

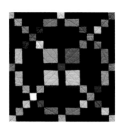

Although I don't use solid fabrics in my scrap quilts, Maureen does here in her treatment of "Burgoyne Surrounded," in which she uses a black background combined with light and bright solids. The solid fabrics give a completely different look to a traditional favorite pattern. She proves the rule that you should "never say never."

MATERIALS

Yardage is based on 42"-wide fabric.

8⅜ yards of black solid for background, sashing, outer border, and binding

3⅝ yards *total* assorted light and bright solid fabrics for blocks, sashing squares, and inner border

8 yards of fabric for backing (3 widths pieced crosswise)

91" x 109" piece of batting

CUTTING

Cut all strips across the width of fabric (selvage to selvage).

From the black solid, cut:
5 strips, 15½" x 42"; crosscut into 49 sashing strips, 3½" x 15½"

10 border strips, 4½" x 42"

22 strips, 3½" x 42"; crosscut into:
    160 pieces, 2½" x 3½"
    80 pieces, 3½" x 5½"

10 strips, 2½" x 42"; cut each strip in half to yield 20 strips, 2½" x 21"

31 strips, 1½" x 42"; cut each strip in half to yield 62 strips, 1½" x 21" (1 strip will be extra)

From the light and bright solid colors, cut a total of:
10 binding strips, 2¼" x 42" (use an assortment of fabrics)

26 strips, 2½" x 21"

66 strips, 1½" x 21"

9 border strips, 1½" x 42" (use an assortment of fabrics)

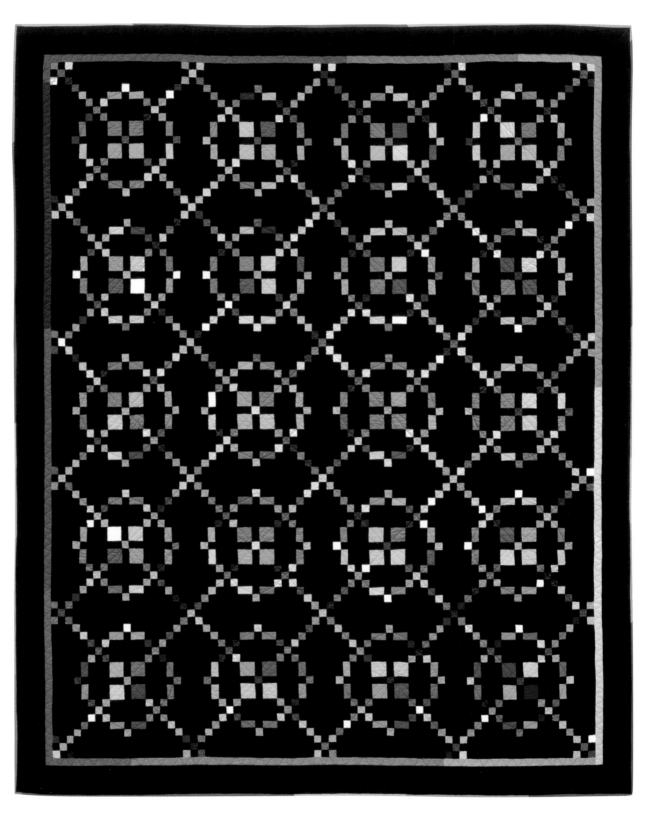

By Maureen McGee, 1993, Lansing, Kansas.

MAKING THE UNITS

The blocks and sashing corner squares are assembled from five different strip-pieced units. After sewing each seam, press the seam allowances in the direction indicated by the arrows.

strip-set units 1 and 2

1. Sew 1½"-wide black and solid-colored strips together along their long edges to make strip-set units as shown. Make the number of units indicated for each color combination. Cut the units into the number of 1½"-wide segments shown.

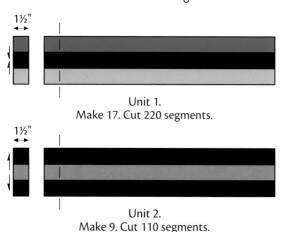

Unit 1.
Make 17. Cut 220 segments.

Unit 2.
Make 9. Cut 110 segments.

2. Randomly sew the segments together as shown to make nine-patch units, mixing segments from different strip-set units. Make 110 blocks, reserving 30 blocks for the sashing corner squares.

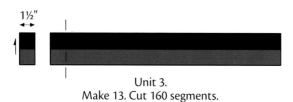

Nine-patch unit.
Make 110.

strip-set unit 3

1. Sew pairs of 1½"-wide black and solid-colored strips together along their long edges to make 13 strip-set units. Cut the units into 160 segments, 1½" wide.

Unit 3.
Make 13. Cut 160 segments.

2. Mixing segments from different strip-set units, sew the segments together in pairs to make 80 four-patch units as shown.

Four-patch unit.
Make 80.

strip-set units 4 and 5

1. Sew two 2½"-wide solid-colored strips and one 1½"-wide black strip together along their long edges to make unit 4. Sew two 2½"-wide black strips and one 1½"-wide solid-colored strip together as shown to make unit 5. Make the number of units indicated for each color combination.

Unit 4.
Make 13.

Unit 5.
Make 10.

2. Cut the unit 4 strip sets into 80 segments, 1½" wide, cutting six or seven segments from each unit to get a variety of fabric combinations. Reserve the remaining strip-set units.

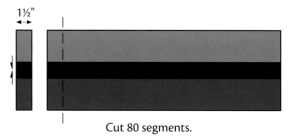

Cut 80 segments.

3. Cut the unit 5 strip sets into 80 segments, 1½" wide, cutting eight segments from each unit to get a variety of fabric combinations. Reserve the remaining strip-set units.

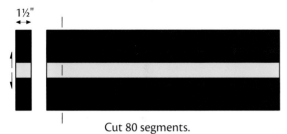

Cut 80 segments.

4. Sew one unit 4 segment and one unit 5 segment together as shown to make block units. Make 80.

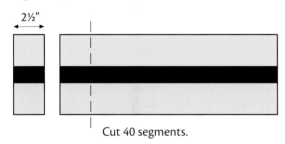

Make 80.

5. Cut the reserved unit 4 strip sets into 40 segments, 2½" wide.

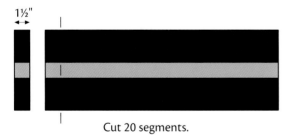

Cut 40 segments.

6. Cut the reserved unit 5 strip sets into 20 segments, 1½" wide.

Cut 20 segments.

7. Sew two unit 4 segments and one unit 5 segment together as shown to make 20 center-block units.

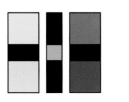

Make 20.

MAKING THE BLOCKS

Lay out four nine-patch units, four four-patch units, four block units, one center-block unit, eight 2½" x 3½" black rectangles, and four 3½" x 5½" black rectangles as shown. Sew the units together in rows, and then sew the rows together and press. Make a total of 20 blocks.

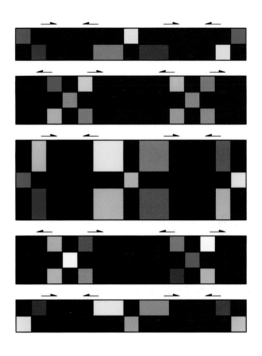

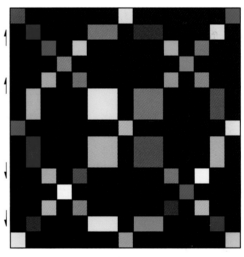

Make 20.

ASSEMBLING THE QUILT TOP

1. Using the reserved nine-patch units and the 3½"-wide black sashing strips, sew five units and four sashing strips together as shown, beginning and ending with a nine-patch unit. Make a total of six sashing rows.

Make 6.

2. Arrange the blocks into five rows of four blocks each. Sew the blocks together in rows with sashing strips between each block. Sew a sashing strip to both ends of each row. Make five block rows.

Make 5.

3. Sew the block rows and sashing rows together to form the quilt top, beginning and ending with a sashing row.

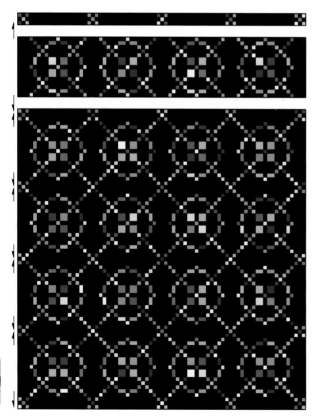

4. Refer to "Borders with Butted Corners" on page 105 to measure, cut, and sew the 1½"-wide solid-colored inner-border strips, and then the 4½"-wide black outer-border strips to the quilt top. Press all seam allowances toward the just-added border strips.

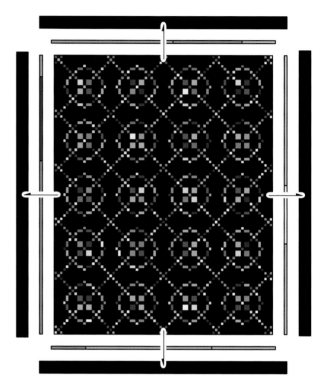

FINISHING THE QUILT

1. Layer the quilt with batting and backing; baste.

2. Quilt as desired, or follow the quilting suggestion on the facing page.

3. Referring to "Binding" on page 108, prepare the binding and sew it to the quilt. Add a label.

Quilt layout

Quilting diagram

crazy chain

Finished quilt size: 89½" x 107½" ✳ Finished block size: 9" ✳ Number of Eccentric Star blocks: 49
Number of Chain blocks: 50

Some years ago, I moved my fabric from one part of the house to another with help from my son Ted. When we were finished, he announced that I couldn't buy any more blue fabric, since he had just moved about 24 cubic feet of blues. This quilt made almost no dent in that collection! The simple Star block is a variation of an Eccentric Star block, and the alternate block forms a chain—an easy segue to the name "Crazy Chain."

MATERIALS
Yardage is based on 42"-wide fabric.
6½ yards of light print for background
3⅝ yards *total* of assorted blue prints for blocks
2⅛ yards of dark blue fabric for border and binding
8½ yards of fabric for backing (3 widths pieced crosswise)
95" x 113" piece of batting

CUTTING
Cut all strips across the width of fabric (selvage to selvage).

From the light print, cut:
49 strips, 3½" x 42"; crosscut into:
    98 rectangles, 3½" x 4½"
    396 squares, 3½" x 3½"
20 strips, 2" x 42"; crosscut into 40 strips, 2" x 21"

From the assorted blue prints, cut a total of:
45 strips, 3½" x 21"; crosscut into:
    98 rectangles, 3½" x 4½"
    99 squares, 3½" x 3½"
20 strips, 2" x 42"; crosscut into 40 strips, 2" x 21"

From the dark blue fabric, cut:
10 border strips, 4½" x 42"
11 binding strips, 2¼" x 42"

By Sally Schneider, 2000, Breinigsville, Pennsylvania.

Quilted by Kari Lane. From the collection of Tyler and Amy McLaughlin.

MAKING THE ECCENTRIC STAR BLOCKS

After sewing each seam, press the seam allowances in the direction indicated by the arrows.

1. Referring to "Method One" on page 99, layer a 3½" x 4½" light print rectangle and a blue rectangle right sides together and draw 45° lines from opposite corners on the wrong side of the light rectangle. Sew on both drawn lines, and then cut the rectangles apart between the lines. Press the seam allowances toward the darker fabric. Make 196 triangle squares.

Make 196.

2. Lay out four triangle squares, four 3½" light print squares, and one 3½" blue square in a nine-patch arrangement. Sew the pieces together in rows, and then sew the rows together to complete an Eccentric Star block. You may make all four triangles squares in a block from the same fabric or you may mix them up. (I prefer mixing them up!) Make a total of 49 blocks.

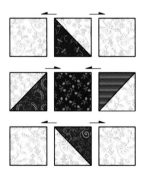

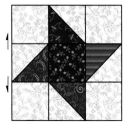

Make 49.

MAKING THE CHAIN BLOCKS

After sewing each seam, press the seam allowances in the direction indicated by the arrows.

1. Pair each 2"-wide blue strip with a 2"-wide light print strip. Sew them together along the long edges. Make a total of 40 strip sets. Cut the strip sets into 400 segments, 2" wide.

Make 40 strip sets.
Cut 400 segments.

2. Sew two segments together as shown to make a four-patch unit. Make 200 units.

Make 200.

3. Lay out four four-patch units, four 3½" light print squares, and one 3½" blue square in a nine-patch arrangement. Sew the pieces together in rows, and then sew the rows together to complete a Chain block. Make a total of 50 blocks.

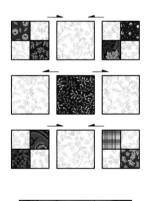

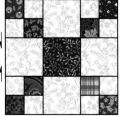

Make 50.

ASSEMBLING THE QUILT TOP

1. Lay out the blocks in 11 rows of 9 blocks each, starting with a Chain block in the outer corners and alternating with the Eccentric Star blocks. Sew the blocks together into rows, pressing the seam allowances toward the Chain blocks. Then sew the rows together and press the seam allowances in one direction.

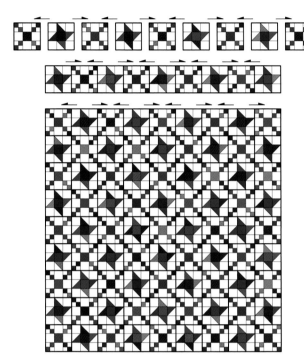

Quilt layout

2. Refer to "Borders with Butted Corners" on page 105 to measure, cut, and sew the 4½"-wide

blue outer-border strips to the quilt top. Press all seam allowances toward the outer-border strips.

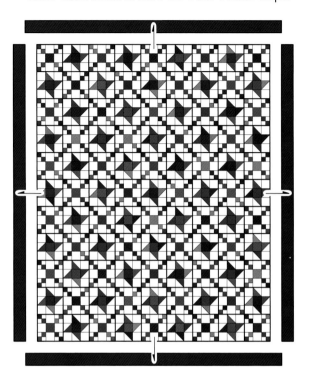

FINISHING THE QUILT

1. Layer the quilt top with backing and batting; baste.

2. Quilt as desired, or follow the quilting suggestion below.

Quilting diagram

3. Referring to "Binding" on page 108, prepare the binding and sew it to the quilt. Add a label.

dawn stars

Finished quilt size: 50¾" x 63½" ✳ Finished block size: 9" ✳ Number of Morning Star blocks: 6
Number of Nine Patch Star blocks: 12

A combination of two star blocks—a Morning Star variation and a Nine Patch Star—gives more life to a quilt than just a single star pattern. The purple stars and peach background bring southwestern early mornings to life, while the greens and turquoises reflect the desert and surrounding mountains of New Mexico. I have been asked if moving to the Southwest has influenced my color choices; I guess my answer is yes—it sure has! I used the fabric-menu technique to determine fabric choices for this quilt.

MATERIALS

Yardage is based on 42"-wide fabric.

1⅜ yards of peach print for background

1⅜ yards of dark purple print for outer border and binding

1 yard of medium purple print for setting triangles

½ yard *total* of 6 assorted purple prints for Evening Star blocks

⅜ yard of green print for inner border

⅜ yard *total* of 12 assorted orange prints for Nine Patch Star blocks

¼ yard *total* of 6 assorted green prints for Evening Star blocks

¼ yard *total* of assorted turquoise prints for Nine Patch Star blocks

3⅜ yards of fabric for backing (2 widths pieced crosswise)

55" x 67" piece of batting

CUTTING

Cut all strips across the width of fabric (selvage to selvage).

From the peach print, cut:
11 strips, 3½" x 42"; crosscut into 120 squares, 3½" x 3½"
3 strips, 2" x 42"; crosscut into 48 squares, 2" x 2"

From *each* of the 6 assorted purple prints, cut:
8 rectangles, 2" x 3½" (48 total)
1 square, 3½" x 3½" (6 total)

From *each* of the 6 assorted green prints, cut:
8 squares, 2" x 2" (48 total)

From *each* of the 12 assorted orange prints, cut:
8 squares, 2" x 2" (96 total)

From the assorted turquoise prints, cut a total of:
12 squares, 3½" x 3½"

Continued on page 42.

By Sally Schneider, 2008, Albuquerque, New Mexico.

Quilted by Leona VanLeeuwen.

From the medium purple print, cut:

2 strips, 14½" x 42"; crosscut into:

    3 squares, 14½" x 14½"; cut each square twice diagonally to yield 12 setting triangles (2 will be extra)

    2 squares, 9" x 9"; cut each square once diagonally to yield 4 corner triangles

From the green print for inner border, cut:

5 strips, 2" x 42"

From the dark purple print, cut:

6 border strips, 5" x 42"

6 binding strips, 2¼" x 42"

MAKING THE MORNING STAR BLOCKS

Directions are for making one block. Repeat to make a total of six blocks. After sewing each seam, press the seam allowances in the direction indicated by the arrows.

1. Referring to "Making Folded Corners" on page 100, place a 2" peach square on one end of a purple rectangle. Make a total of eight matching units; sew four with the seams facing in one direction and four with the seams in the opposite direction. Trim and press.

    Make 4.   Make 4.

2. In the same manner, sew matching green squares to the opposite end of each rectangle from step 1. Be sure to stitch the seams in the same direction as the peach squares.

    Make 4.   Make 4.

3. Sew two units from step 2 together as shown, pressing the seam allowance open. Make four side units.

    Make 4.

4. Lay out the side units from step 3, one 3½" purple square, and four 3½" peach squares in a nine-patch arrangement. Sew the pieces together in rows, and then sew rows together to complete a Morning Star block. Make a total of six blocks.

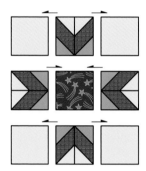 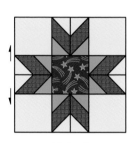

    Make 6.

MAKING THE NINE PATCH STAR BLOCKS

Directions are for one block. Repeat to make a total of 12 blocks. After sewing each seam, press the seam allowances in the direction indicated by the arrows.

1. Referring to "Making Folded Corners," sew matching orange squares to adjacent corners of a 3½" peach square. Trim and press. Make four matching folded-corner units.

    Make 4.

2. Lay out the units from step 1, one 3½" turquoise square, and four 3½" peach squares in a nine-patch arrangement. Sew the pieces together in rows, and then sew rows together to complete a Nine Patch Star block. Make a total of 12 blocks.

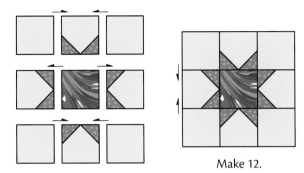

Make 12.

ASSEMBLING THE QUILT TOP

For detailed instructions, refer to "Quilts Set Diagonally" on page 103.

1. Lay out the Nine Patch Star blocks, the Morning Star blocks, and the medium purple side and corner triangles in diagonal rows. When you are satisfied with the arrangement, sew the blocks and side triangles together into rows and press.

2. Sew the rows together, adding the corner triangles last, and press. The setting triangles were cut a bit oversized for easier cutting and piecing. Trim and square up the quilt top, making sure to leave ¼" beyond the points of all blocks for seam allowances.

Quilt layout

3. Refer to "Borders with Butted Corners" on page 105 to measure, cut, and sew the 2"-wide green inner-border strips, and then the 5"-wide dark purple outer-border strips to the quilt top. Press all seam allowances toward the outer-border strips.

FINISHING THE QUILT

1. Layer the quilt top with backing and batting; baste.

2. Quilt as desired, or follow the quilting suggestion below.

Quilting diagram

3. Referring to "Binding" on page 108, prepare the binding and sew it to the quilt. Add a label.

fireworks

There was a method to my madness when I made this quilt. I decided to use the fabric-menu technique on page 8 for choosing the fabrics. With this method, I assigned either colors or values to different parts of the quilt. The result is an exciting luminescence.

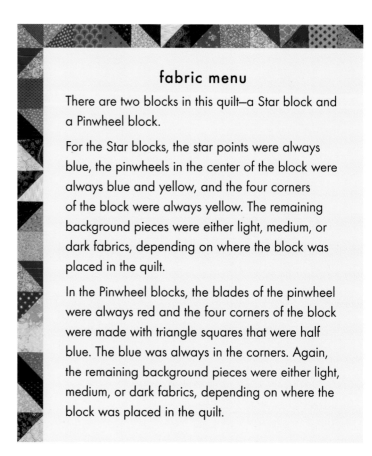

fabric menu

There are two blocks in this quilt—a Star block and a Pinwheel block.

For the Star blocks, the star points were always blue, the pinwheels in the center of the block were always blue and yellow, and the four corners of the block were always yellow. The remaining background pieces were either light, medium, or dark fabrics, depending on where the block was placed in the quilt.

In the Pinwheel blocks, the blades of the pinwheel were always red and the four corners of the block were made with triangle squares that were half blue. The blue was always in the corners. Again, the remaining background pieces were either light, medium, or dark fabrics, depending on where the block was placed in the quilt.

MATERIALS

Yardage is based on 42"-wide fabric. All the pieces in this quilt are cut from 3½" strips. For those of you who want to use just a few colors, yardages are as follows.

2⅛ yards *total* of assorted dark prints for blocks

2 yards *total* of assorted blue prints for blocks

1¼ yards *total* of assorted yellow prints for blocks

1¼ yards *total* of assorted medium prints for blocks

⅝ yard *total* of assorted red prints for blocks

¼ yard *total* of assorted light prints for blocks

⅝ yard of red print for binding

5½ yards of fabric for backing (2 widths pieced lengthwise)

66" x 90" piece of batting

By Sally Schneider, 1990, Puyallup, Washington.

CUTTING

Cut all strips across the width of fabric (selvage to selvage).

From the assorted yellow prints, cut a total of:
36 rectangles, 3½" x 4½"

72 squares, 3½" x 3½"

From the assorted blue prints, cut a total of:
142 rectangles, 3½" x 4½"

From the assorted dark prints, cut a total of:
84 rectangles, 3½" x 4½"

80 squares, 3½" x 3½"

From the assorted medium prints, cut a total of:
48 rectangles, 3½" x 4½"

48 squares, 3½" x 3½"

From the assorted light prints, cut a total of:
8 rectangles, 3½" x 4½"

8 squares, 3½" x 3½"

From the assorted red prints, cut a total of:
34 rectangles, 3½" x 4½"

From the red print for binding, cut:
8 strips, 2¼" x 42"

MAKING THE BLOCKS

After sewing each seam, press the seam allowances in the direction indicated by the arrows.

1. Referring to "Method One" on page 99, layer a blue rectangle and a yellow rectangle right sides together and draw 45° lines from opposite corners on the wrong side of the yellow rectangle. Sew on both drawn lines, and then cut apart between the lines. Press the seam allowances toward the darker fabric. Make 72 triangle squares.

Make 72.

2. Repeat step 1, sewing rectangles together in the combinations listed below to make the number of triangle squares indicated for each color combination:

   - 64 pairs of blue and dark print rectangles to make 128 triangle squares

   - 36 pairs of blue and medium print rectangles to make 72 triangle squares

   - 6 pairs of blue and light print rectangles to make 12 triangle squares

   - 2 pairs of red and light print rectangles to make 4 triangle squares

   - 12 pairs of red and medium print rectangles to make 24 triangle squares

   - 20 pairs of red and dark print rectangles to make 40 triangle squares

Make 128.   Make 72.   Make 12.

Make 4.   Make 24.   Make 40.

3. Lay out the triangle squares and 3½" squares as shown for each color combination. Sew the units in each row together, and then sew the rows together to complete the block. Make the number of blocks indicated for each color combination.

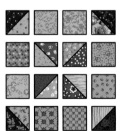 

Block 1.
Make 6.

Block 2.
Make 10.

Block 3.
Make 1.

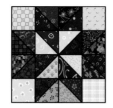

Block 4.
Make 6.

Block 5.
Make 2.

Block 6.
Make 4.

Block 7.
Make 2.

Block 8.
Make 4.

ASSEMBLING THE QUILT TOP

1. Arrange the completed blocks as shown in the layout map.

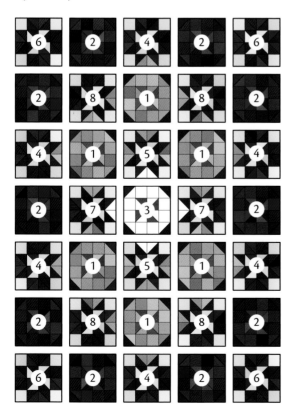

Layout map

2. Sew the blocks together in rows, pressing the seam allowances in opposite directions from one row to the next. Then sew the rows together and press the seam allowances in one direction.

   I chose not to add borders to my quilt, but if you prefer them, see "Borders with Butted Corners" on page 105 for guidance on adding borders.

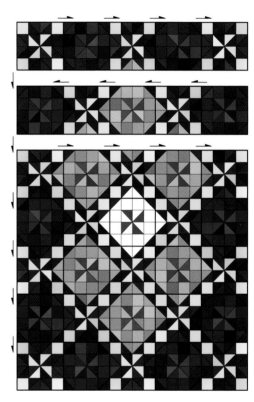

FINISHING THE QUILT

1. Layer the quilt with batting and backing; baste.

2. Quilt as desired.

3. Referring to "Binding" on page 108, prepare the binding and sew it to the quilt. Add a label.

for my dad

Finished quilt size: 56½" x 64" ✳ Finished block size: 7½" ✳ Number of blocks: 42

A simple pattern of squares and rectangles, the Catherine Wheels block used here was inspired by an antique quilt top owned by Cathy Hansen. I made this quilt as a Christmas gift for my father.

MATERIALS
Yardage is based on 42"-wide fabric.

1⅝ yards of light print for background

1⅝ yards *total* of assorted dark prints for blocks

⅞ yard of dark print for outer border

½ yard of dark blue print for inner border

⅝ yard of red print for binding

3¾ yards of fabric for backing (2 widths pieced crosswise)

62" x 69" piece of batting

CUTTING
Cut all strips across the width of fabric (selvage to selvage).

From the assorted dark prints, cut a total of:
51 strips, 2" x 21"

From the light print, cut:
9 strips, 5" x 42"; crosscut into 168 rectangles, 2" x 5"

3 strips, 2" x 42"; crosscut into 42 squares, 2" x 2"

From the dark blue print for inner border, cut:
6 strips, 2" x 42"

From the dark print for outer border, cut:
6 strips, 4½" x 42"

From the red print, cut:
7 strips, 2¼" x 42"

By Sally Schneider, 1992, Puyallup, Washington.

From the collection of William George.

MAKING THE BLOCKS

1. Sew three 2"-wide dark print strips together along their long edges to make a strip set. Press the seam allowances toward the center strip. Make 17 strip sets. Cut the strip sets into 168 segments, 2" wide. The segments should measure 2" x 5".

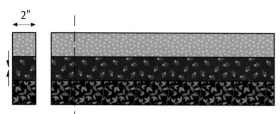

Make 17 strip sets.
Cut 168 segments.

2. Sew each segment from step 1 to a light print rectangle as shown to make a rectangle unit. Press the seam allowances toward the light rectangle. Make 168.

Make 168.

3. Sew one light print square and one rectangle unit from step 2 together as shown, stopping in the center of the square. Press the seam allowance toward the center square.

4. Matching the seams, sew a rectangle unit to the unit from step 3 as shown; press. Add rectangle units in a clockwise direction only. *Adding the units in the opposite direction will make the block appear to twist backward.*

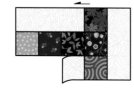

5. Sew a third rectangle unit to the unit from step 4, matching seams; press.

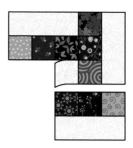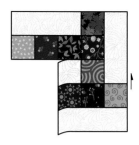

6. Sew a fourth rectangle unit to the block; press. Matching seams, sew the center-square seam closed, starting at the center square and stitching to the block's outer edge, to complete the block. Repeat to make a total of 42 blocks.

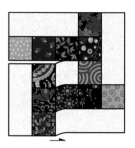

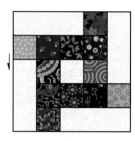

Make 42.

ASSEMBLING THE QUILT TOP

1. Lay out the blocks in seven rows of six blocks each. When you are satisfied with the arrangement, sew the blocks together in rows. Press the seam allowances in opposite directions from one row to the next. Then sew the rows together and press the seam allowances in one direction.

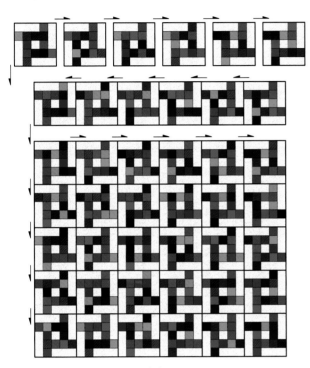

Quilt layout

2. Refer to "Borders with Butted Corners" on page 105 to measure, cut, and sew the 2"-wide inner-border strips, and then the 4½"-wide outer-border strips to the quilt top. Press all seam allowances toward the just-added border strips.

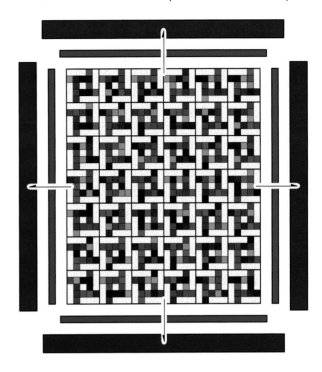

FINISHING THE QUILT

1. Layer the quilt with batting and backing; baste.

2. Quilt as desired.

3. Referring to "Binding" on page 108, prepare the binding and sew it to the quilt. Add a label.

friendship stars

Finished quilt size: 69" x 85" ✳ Finished block size: 4" ✳ Number of Four Patch blocks: 143

I collected squares from students and fellow guild members for more than a year to stitch into this quilt. The large variety of background fabrics weaves a rich tapestry, although you can make the quilt using just one background fabric, or a mix of fat quarters or scraps.

MATERIALS

Yardage is based on 42"-wide fabric.

3⅜ yards *total* of assorted dark prints for blocks

3¼ yards *total* of assorted light prints for background

1 yard of dark print for outer border

⅜ yard of rust print for inner border

⅝ yard of dark blue print for binding

5½ yards of fabric for backing (2 widths pieced lengthwise)

74" x 90" piece of batting

CUTTING

Cut all strips across the width of fabric (selvage to selvage).

From the assorted light prints, cut a total of:
18 strips, 4½" x 42"; crosscut into 142 squares, 4½" x 4½"

20 strips, 2½" x 21"

From the assorted dark prints, cut a total of:
44 strips, 2½" x 42"; crosscut into:

    52 strips, 2½" x 21"

    284 squares, 2½" x 2½"

From the rust print for inner border, cut:
8 strips, 1½" x 42"

From the dark print for outer border, cut:
8 strips, 3¾" x 42"

From the dark blue print, cut:
8 strips, 2¼" x 42"

By Sally Schneider, 1993, Puyallup, Washington.

MAKING THE BLOCKS

1. Referring to "Making Folded Corners" on page 100, sew 2½" dark print squares to adjacent corners of each 4½" light print square. Trim and press. Make a total of 142 folded-corner units.

Make 142.

savvy charm squares

If you ask your friends to do this first step, you'll have a good chance to increase the variety of fabrics used in your quilt! Have them sign, date, and write their hometown on the pieces.

2. Sew pairs of dark print and light print strips together along their long edges to make 20 strip sets. Press the seam allowances toward the dark print strips. Cut the strip sets into 160 segments, 2½" wide.

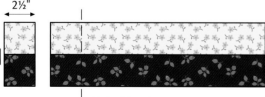

2½"

Make 20 strip sets.
Cut 160 segments.

3. Sew the segments together in pairs, matching the seam intersections, and press. Make a total of 80 Four Patch blocks.

Four Patch block.
Make 80.

4. Sew the remaining dark print strips together in pairs along their long edges. Press the seam allowances toward the darker strip. Make a total of 16 strip sets. Cut these strip sets into 126 segments, 2½" wide.

2½"

Make 16 strip sets.
Cut 126 segments.

5. Randomly sew the segments together in pairs, matching the seam intersection, and press. Make a total of 63 Four Patch blocks.

Four Patch block.
Make 63.

ASSEMBLING THE QUILT TOP

1. Lay out the folded-corner units and Four Patch blocks in rows as shown above right. There are four different row configurations. You'll need five each of rows 1, 2, and 3, and four of row 4. Each row contains 15 units or blocks. Within each row, rotate alternating folded-corner units 180° and rotate Four Patch blocks 90°.

    Row 1: Begin and end with a Four Patch block.

    Row 2: Begin and end with a folded-corner unit.

    Row 3: Begin and end with a Four Patch block. (Note that this is simply row 1 turned upside down.)

Row 4: Begin and end with a folded-corner unit.

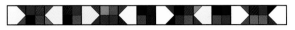

Row 1.
Make 5.

Row 2.
Make 5.

Row 3.
Make 5.

Row 4.
Make 4.

2. Sew the blocks together in rows, pressing the seam allowances in opposite directions from one row to the next. Sew the rows together, referring to the layout diagram for placement guidance. Press the seam allowances in one direction.

Quilt layout

3. Refer to "Borders with Butted Corners" on page 105 to measure, cut, and sew the 1½"-wide rust inner-border strips, and then the 3¾" dark print outer-border strips to the quilt top. Press all seam allowances toward the just-added strips.

FINISHING THE QUILT

1. Layer the quilt with batting and backing; baste.

2. Quilt as desired.

3. Referring to "Binding" on page 108, prepare the binding and sew it to the quilt. Add a label.

good fences
make good neighbors

Finished quilt size: 81¼" x 95½" ✳ Finished block size: 10" ✳ Number of Pinwheel blocks: 50

When I first saw this design in a photograph, it was done in Amish colors and looked quite complex and difficult to make. Further analysis, however, showed it to be a simple block in a diagonal setting. The name of the quilt comes from Robert Frost's poem *Mending Wall*, and refers to the scrap pinwheels kept separate by the Rail Fence strip between each group of colorful pinwheels.

MATERIALS

Yardage is based on 42"-wide fabric.

1⅞ yards *total* of assorted light prints for blocks

1⅞ yards *total* of assorted dark prints for blocks

2⅞ yards of navy print for Rail Fence strips and borders

1⅓ yards of red print for Rail Fence strips

1½ yards of light print for setting triangles

¾ yard of red print for binding

7½ yards of backing (3 widths pieced crosswise)

86" x 101" piece of batting

CUTTING

Cut all strips across the width of fabric (selvage to selvage).

From the assorted dark prints, cut a total of:
20 strips, 3" x 42"; crosscut into 200 rectangles, 3" x 4"

From the assorted light prints, cut a total of:
20 strips, 3" x 42"; crosscut into 200 rectangles, 3" x 4"

From the red print, cut:
4 strips, 10½" x 42"; crosscut into 50 rectangles, 3" x 10½"

From the navy print, cut:
4 strips, 10½" x 42"; crosscut into 50 rectangles, 3" x 10½"
9 border strips, 5½" x 42"

From the light print for setting triangles, cut:
3 strips, 16" x 42"; crosscut into:

> 5 squares, 16" x 16"; cut each square twice diagonally to yield 20 setting triangles (2 will be extra)

> 2 squares, 10" x 10"; cut each square once diagonally to yield 4 corner triangles

From the red print for binding, cut:
9 strips, 2¼" x 42"

By Sally Schneider, 2008, Albuquerque, New Mexico.

Quilted by Leona VanLeeuwen.

MAKING THE BLOCKS

After sewing each seam, press the seam allowances in the direction indicated by the arrows.

1. Referring to "Method One" on page 99, layer a light print rectangle and a dark print rectangle right sides together and draw 45° lines from opposite corners on the wrong side of the light rectangle. Sew on both drawn lines, and then cut the rectangles apart between the lines. Press the seam allowances toward the darker fabric. Repeat to make four matching triangle squares. Make a total of 400 triangle squares.

Make 4 matching
triangle squares.

2. Lay out a set of four matching triangle squares in a four-patch arrangement. Make sure you keep the light and dark triangles always rotating in the same direction; otherwise some of your pinwheels will spin in the opposite direction. Sew the triangle squares together in pairs, and then sew the pairs together to complete the pinwheel units. Make a total of 100 pinwheel units.

Make 100.

3. Sew pinwheel units together in pairs to make 50 block centers.

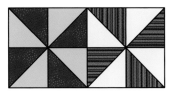

Make 50.

4. Sew a navy rectangle to one long side of each block center, and then sew a red rectangle to the opposite side. Make 50 blocks measuring 10½" square.

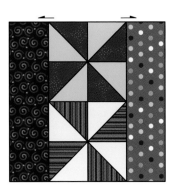

Make 50.

ASSEMBLING THE QUILT TOP

For detailed instructions, refer to "Quilts Set Diagonally" on page 103.

1. Lay out the blocks and the light print side and corner setting triangles as shown in the quilt layout diagram on the facing page. Make sure to arrange the blocks to keep the lines of color zigzagging across the quilt top.

2. When you are satisfied with the block arrangement, sew the blocks and side triangles together into diagonal rows. Press the seam allowances in opposite directions from one row to the next.

Sew the rows together. Add the corner triangles last and press. The setting triangles were cut a bit oversized for easier cutting and piecing. Trim and square up the quilt top, making sure to leave ¼" beyond the points of all blocks for seam allowances.

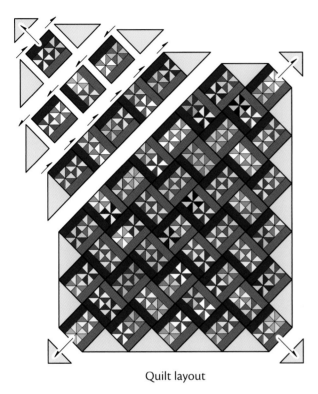

Quilt layout

3. Refer to "Borders with Butted Corners" on page 105 to measure, cut, and sew the 5½"-wide navy outer-border strips to the quilt top.

Press all seam allowances toward the outer-border strips.

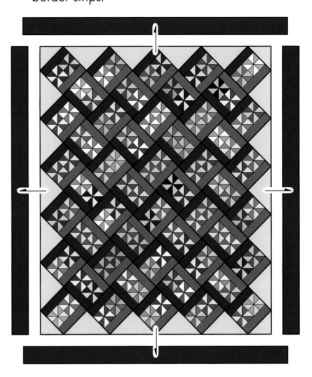

FINISHING THE QUILT

1. Layer the quilt top with backing and batting; baste.

2. Quilt as desired, or follow the quilting suggestion below.

Quilting diagram

3. Referring to "Binding" on page 108, prepare the binding and sew it to the quilt. Add a label.

interweave

Finished quilt size: 68½" x 88½" ✳ Finished block size: 10" ✳ Number of blocks: 48

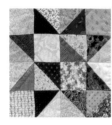

By itself, the block used for this quilt doesn't look like much more than a jumble of light and dark triangles. But when the blocks are set together and rotated in different directions, they form a pattern that creates an overall woven effect through the interplay of light and dark fabrics.

MATERIALS

Yardage is based on 42"-wide fabric.

4½ yards *total* of assorted light prints for blocks

2¼ yards *total* of assorted dark prints for blocks

1½ yards of dark blue fabric for outer border and binding

½ yard of teal fabric for inner border

5¾ yards of fabric for backing (2 widths pieced lengthwise)

74" x 94" piece of batting

CUTTING

Cut all strips across the width of fabric (selvage to selvage).

From the assorted light prints, cut a total of:
96 strips, 3" x 21"; crosscut into:
    240 rectangles, 3" x 4"
    288 squares, 3" x 3"

From the assorted dark prints, cut a total of:
48 strips, 3" x 21"; crosscut into 240 rectangles, 3" x 4"

From the teal fabric, cut:
8 strips, 1½" x 42"

From the dark blue fabric, cut:
8 border strips, 3½" x 42"
9 binding strips, 2¼" x 42"

By Sally Schneider, 1993, Puyallup, Washington.

MAKING THE BLOCKS

1. Referring to "Method One" on page 99, layer a light print rectangle and a dark print rectangle right sides together and draw 45° lines from opposite corners on the wrong side of the light rectangle. Sew on both drawn lines, and then cut the rectangles apart between the lines. Press the seam allowances toward the darker fabric. Make 480 triangle squares.

Make 480.

2. To assemble one block, select six light print squares and 10 triangle squares from step 1. Lay out the squares in four rows of four squares each, making sure to arrange them as shown to create a light diagonal area. Sew the squares together in rows, and then sew the rows together, pressing the seam allowances as indicated. Repeat to make a total of 48 blocks.

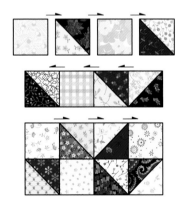

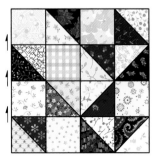

Make 48.

ASSEMBLING THE QUILT TOP

1. Lay out the blocks in eight rows of six blocks each as shown in the quilt layout diagram. You'll need four each of rows 1 and 2. Notice that the blocks are rotated from one block to the next and from row to row; finding the light area in each block will help you orient the blocks properly. Sew the blocks together in rows, pressing the seam allowances in opposite directions from one row to the next.

2. Sew the rows together and press the seam allowances in one direction.

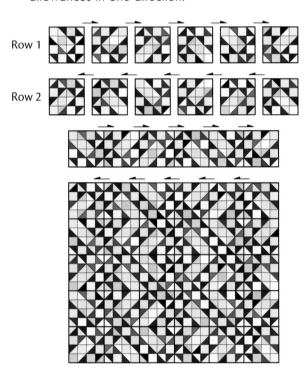

Quilt layout

3. Refer to "Borders with Butted Corners" on page 105 to measure, cut, and sew the 1½"-wide teal inner-border strips, and then the 3½"-wide dark blue outer-border strips to the quilt top. Press all seam allowances toward the just-added strips.

FINISHING THE QUILT

1. Layer the quilt top with backing and batting; baste.

2. Quilt as desired, or follow the quilting suggestion at right.

3. Referring to "Binding" on page 108, prepare the binding and sew it to the quilt. Add a label.

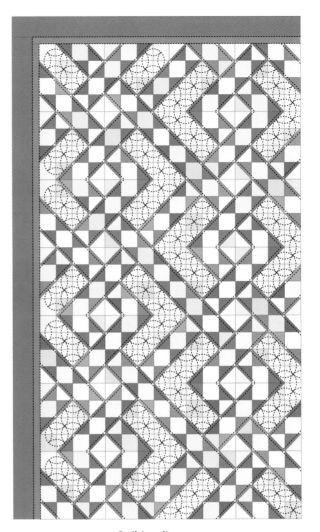

Quilting diagram

joseph's coat

Finished quilt size: 60¼" x 77½" ❋ Finished block size: 14¼" ❋ Number of blocks: 12

A collection of my favorite Civil War—era reproduction fabrics and a photo of a quilt that I just had to make were the starting places for this handsome quilt.

MATERIALS

Yardage is based on 42"-wide fabric.

2¼ yards of dark blue print for sashing and border

2¼ yards *total* of assorted light prints for blocks

1⅞ yards *total* of assorted dark prints for blocks

¼ yard of red print for sashing corner squares

⅝ yard of dark red print for binding

5⅛ yards of fabric for backing (2 widths pieced lengthwise)

66" x 83" piece of batting

CUTTING

Cut all strips across the width of fabric (selvage to selvage).

From the assorted light prints, cut a total of:

12 squares, 4⅛" x 4⅛"; cut each square twice diagonally to yield 48 quarter-square triangles

72 squares, 3¾" x 3¾"; cut each square once diagonally to yield 144 half-square triangles

48 squares, 3¼" x 3¼"

48 rectangles, 2½" x 4½"

48 squares, 2½" x 2½"

From the assorted dark prints, cut a total of:

12 squares, 4½" x 4½"

144 squares, 2⅞" x 2⅞"; cut each square once diagonally to yield 288 half-square triangles

96 squares, 2½" x 2½"

From the dark blue print, cut:

2 strips, 14¾" x 42"; crosscut into 17 strips, 3½" x 14¾"

7 border strips, 6" x 42"

From the red print, cut:

6 squares, 3½" x 3½"

From the dark red print for binding, cut:

8 strips, 2¼" x 42"

By Sally Schneider, 2000, Breinigsville, Pennsylvania.

Quilted by Kari Lane.

MAKING THE BLOCKS

Directions are for making one block. Repeat to make a total of 12 blocks. After sewing each seam, press the seam allowances in the direction indicated by the arrows.

1. Referring to "Making Folded Corners" on page 100, sew a 2½" dark print square to one end of a light print rectangle. Trim and press. Sew another dark print square to the opposite end of the rectangle with the seam going in the opposite direction to complete the star point. Trim and press. Make four star-point units.

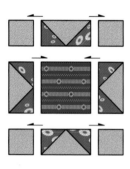

Make 4.

2. Lay out four star-point units, four 2½" light print squares, and one 4½" dark print square as shown. Sew the pieces together in rows, and then sew the rows together to make the center star.

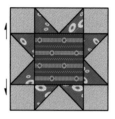

Make 1.

3. Sew four dark print half-square triangles to the sides of a 3¼" light print square as shown. Always sew with the triangle's bias edge on the bottom and the light square on top to keep the bias edge from stretching. Make four.

Make 4.

4. Sew two light print half-square triangles to opposite sides of each unit from step 3. Then sew another triangle to one side as shown. Make four.

Make 4.

5. Sew two dark print half-square triangles to the sides of each unit from step 4. Make four. On two of the units, sew light print quarter-square triangles on both ends of the units as shown.

Make 4.

Make 2.

6. Lay out the center star and the units from step 5. Sew the units together to complete the block. Make a total of 12 blocks.

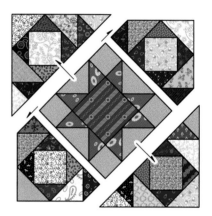

Make 12.

ASSEMBLING THE QUILT TOP

For detailed instructions, refer to "Quilts with Sashing Strips" on page 104.

1. Lay out the blocks in four rows of three blocks each. Sew the blocks together in rows with dark

blue sashing strips between each block. Press the seam allowances toward the sashing strips.

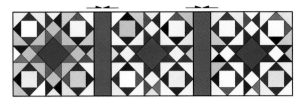

Make 4.

2. Sew three 3½"-wide blue sashing strips and two red squares together as shown, beginning and ending each row with a sashing strip. Make three sashing rows.

Make 3.

3. Sew the block rows and sashing rows together to form the quilt top, beginning and ending with a block row.

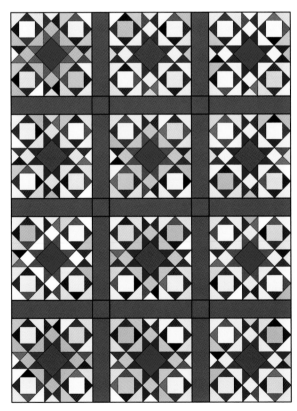

Quilt layout

4. Refer to "Borders with Butted Corners" on page 105 to measure, cut, and sew the 6"-wide blue outer-border strips to the quilt top. Press all seam allowances toward the outer-border strips.

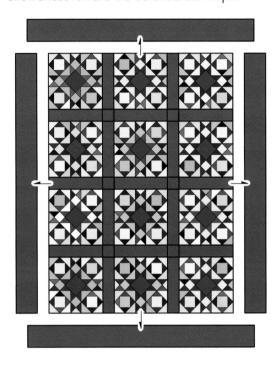

FINISHING THE QUILT

1. Layer the quilt top with backing and batting; baste.

2. Quilt as desired, or follow the quilting suggestion below.

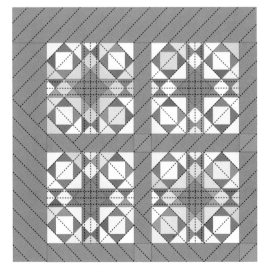

Quilting diagram

3. Referring to "Binding" on page 108, prepare the binding and sew it to the quilt. Add a label.

mt triangled

Finished quilt size: 43½" x 51½" ✳ Finished block size: 4" ✳ Number of blocks: 80

Traditional quilters may recognize the block I call Mary's Triangles as a Shaded Four Patch made of a square, two small triangles, and one large triangle. This versatile block can be arranged in many ways to create patterns well suited to scrap quilts.

While the block is not new, the assembly method given in this book departs from tradition, creating two blocks at a time instead of one. See alternate arrangements on page 71.

MATERIALS

Yardage is based on 42"-wide fabric.

1¼ yards *total* of assorted dark prints for blocks

1¼ yards of dark print for outer border and binding

1 yard *total* of assorted light prints for blocks

¼ yard of red print for inner border

3 yards of fabric for backing (2 widths pieced crosswise)

49" x 57" piece of batting

4½" square of template plastic or a Magic Triangle ruler

CUTTING

Cut all strips across the width of fabric (selvage to selvage).

From the assorted light prints, cut a total of:
40 squares, 2⅞" x 2⅞"
80 rectangles, 2½" x 3½"

From the assorted dark prints, cut a total of:
40 squares, 2⅞" x 2⅞"
40 rectangles, 4½" x 5½"

From the red print, cut:
4 strips, 2" x 42"

From the dark print, cut:
5 border strips, 4½" x 42"
5 binding strips, 2¼" x 42"

By Sally Schneider, 1992, Puyallup, Washington.

MAKING THE BLOCKS

After sewing each seam, press the seam allowances in the direction indicated by the arrows.

1. Referring to "Method Two" on page 100, place light print and dark print squares right sides together, and then draw a diagonal line from corner to corner on the wrong side of each light square. Sew ¼" from each side of the marked line. Cut the squares apart on the line to create two triangle squares. Make a total of 80 triangle squares.

Make 80.

2. Sew each triangle square to a light print rectangle as shown. Make 80.

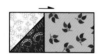

Make 80.

3. Sew pairs of the units from step 2 together as shown. Clip the seam allowances through the seam line in the center so that you can press the seam allowances away from the triangle squares, changing the direction of the seam allowance at the center cut. Make 40.

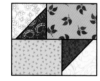

Make 40.

4. Cut the square of template plastic in half diagonally to make a triangle template (or use a Magic Triangle ruler).

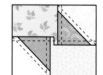

5. Pair each unit from step 3 with a dark print rectangle. Refer to "Making Mary's Triangle Units" on page 101 to mark, sew, and cut the blocks. Make a total of 80 blocks.

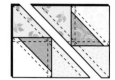

Make 80.

ASSEMBLING THE QUILT TOP

1. Lay out the blocks in 10 rows of eight blocks each as shown in the quilt layout diagram. Notice that the blocks are rotated from one block to the next and from row to row. Or, for other setting options, see page 71. Sew the blocks together in rows, pressing the seam allowances in opposite directions from one row to the next.

2. Sew the rows together and press the seam allowances in one direction.

Quilt layout

3. Refer to "Borders with Butted Corners" on page 105 to measure, cut, and sew the 2"-wide red inner-border strips, and then the 4½"-wide dark print outer-border strips to the quilt top. Press all seam allowances toward the just-added strips.

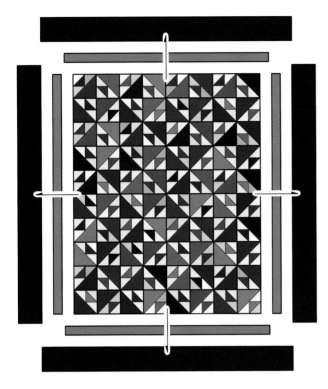

FINISHING THE QUILT

1. Layer the quilt with batting and backing; baste.

2. Quilt as desired.

3. Referring to "Binding" on page 108, prepare the binding and sew it to the quilt. Add a label.

Streak of Lightning variations

Straight Furrows   Star

Straight Furrows variations

This arrangement is called Chain of Friendship and was designed by Yumiko Hirasawa, Yokohama, Japan.

Barn Raising

ocean waves

Finished quilt size: 80½" x 100½" ✳ Finished block size: 20" ✳ Number of blocks: 20

Traditionally, the most challenging part of making the Ocean Waves block is fitting the triangle-square units around the center square. Dividing the center square into quarters and using the Mary's Triangles technique simplifies construction of that section of the block. The Hawaii Quilt Guild made this quilt at a one-day workshop, where we all learned about fabric, techniques, and fellowship.

MATERIALS

Yardage is based on 42"-wide fabric.

4½ yards *total* of assorted light prints for background

4½ yards *total* of assorted dark prints for blocks

2⅜ yards of light background fabric for blocks

¾ yard of dark print for binding

7¾ yards of fabric for backing (3 lengths pieced crosswise)

86" x 106" piece of batting

5½" square of template plastic or a Magic Triangle ruler

CUTTING

Cut all strips across the width of fabric (selvage to selvage).

From the assorted light prints for background, cut a total of:
480 rectangles, 3" x 4"*

From the assorted dark fabrics, cut a total of:
480 rectangles, 3" x 4"*

*You'll use 400 of the rectangles to make triangle squares and the remaining 80 rectangles for the Mary's Triangles units.

From the light background fabric for blocks, cut:
14 strips, 5½" x 42"; crosscut into 80 pieces, 5½" x 6½"

From the dark print for binding, cut:
10 strips, 2¼" x 42"

MAKING THE BLOCKS

After sewing each seam, press the seam allowances in the direction indicated by the arrows.

1. Referring to "Method One" on page 99, layer a light print rectangle and a dark print rectangle right sides together and draw 45° lines from opposite corners on the wrong side of 400 light rectangles. Sew on both drawn lines, and then cut the rectangles apart between the lines.

By the Hawaii Quilt Guild, 1988, Honolulu, Hawaii.

From the collection of Barbara J. Eikmeier.

Press the seam allowances toward the darker fabric. Make a total of 800 triangle squares.

Make 800.

2. Sew one triangle square to each of the remaining light print rectangles as shown to make 80 light units. Sew one triangle square to each of the remaining dark print rectangles to make 80 dark units.

Light unit.
Make 80.

Dark unit.
Make 80.

3. Sew pairs of the light units from step 2 together as shown. Clip the seam allowances through the seam line in the center so that you can press seam allowances away from the triangle squares, changing the direction of the seam allowance at the center cut. Make 40.

Make 40.

4. Sew pairs of the dark units from step 2 together as shown. Clip and press the seam allowances away from the triangle squares in the same manner. Make 40.

Make 40.

5. Cut the square of template plastic in half diagonally to make a triangle template (or use a Magic Triangle ruler).

6. Pair the units from steps 3 and 4 with the 5½" x 6½" background rectangles. Refer to "Making Mary's Triangle Units" on page 101 to mark, sew, and cut the units. Make 80 light and 80 dark Mary's Triangle units.

Make 80.   Make 80.

7. Lay out four triangle squares in a four-patch arrangement, making sure the dark triangles all point in the same direction as shown. Sew the triangle squares together in pairs, and then sew the pairs together to complete the unit. Make 160 units.

Make 160.

8. Lay out two units from step 7 and two Mary's Triangle units (one light and one dark) in a four-patch arrangement as shown. Sew the units together in rows, and then sew the rows together to make a quarter block. Make 80.

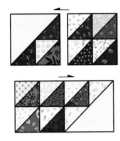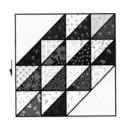

Quarter block.
Make 80.

9. Lay out four quarter blocks, making sure to arrange them as shown so that the dark and light triangles are positioned correctly. Sew the units together in pairs, and then sew the pairs together to complete the block. Make a total of 20 blocks.

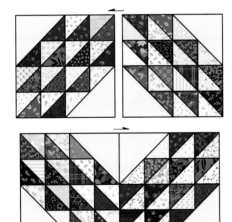

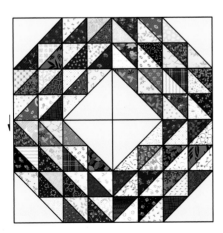

Make 20.

ASSEMBLING THE QUILT TOP

1. Lay out the blocks in five rows of four blocks each as shown in the quilt layout diagram.

2. Sew the blocks together in rows, pressing the seam allowances in opposite directions from one row to the next. Sew the rows together and press the seam allowances in one direction.

Quilt layout

FINISHING THE QUILT

1. Layer the quilt with batting and backing; baste.

2. Quilt as desired.

3. Referring to "Binding" on page 108, prepare the binding and sew it to the quilt. Add a label.

perkiomen valley in the 1930s

Finished quilt size: 70½" x 70½" ✳ Finished block size: 6" ✳ Number of blocks: 100

Sue, the maker of this quilt, loves Nine Patch block variations, and she had been collecting 1930s reproduction fabrics since she began quilting. This design was a perfect marriage of her interests. The pattern name, Perkiomen Valley Nine Patch, refers to the Perkiomen Valley, located in southeastern Pennsylvania, where a great many quilts of this pattern originate.

MATERIALS

Yardage is based on 42"-wide fabric.

2⅝ yards *total* of assorted light fabrics for blocks

2⅝ yards *total* of assorted dark fabrics for blocks

1⅔ yards of green print for outer border and binding

⅜ yard of pink print for inner border

4¾ yards of fabric for backing (2 widths pieced lengthwise or crosswise)

76" x 76" piece of batting

CUTTING

Cut all strips across the width of fabric (selvage to selvage).

From the assorted light fabrics, cut a total of:
150 rectangles, 2½" x 3½"
300 squares, 2½" x 2½"

From the assorted dark fabrics, cut a total of:
150 rectangles, 2½" x 3½"
300 squares, 2½" x 2½"

From the pink print, cut:
7 strips, 1½" x 42"

From the green print, cut:
8 border strips, 4½" x 42"
8 binding strips, 2¼" x 42"

By Susan Phillips, 2000, Fairbanks, Alaska.

MAKING THE BLOCKS

After sewing each seam, press the seam allowances in the direction indicated by the arrows.

1. Referring to "Method One" on page 99, layer a light print rectangle and a dark print rectangle right sides together and draw 45° lines from opposite corners on the wrong side of the light rectangle. Sew on both drawn lines, and then cut the rectangles apart between the lines. Press the seam allowances toward the darker fabric. Make 300 triangle squares.

Make 300.

2. Lay out three light print squares, three dark print squares, and three triangle squares in a nine-patch arrangement as shown. Sew the pieces together in rows, and then sew the rows together to complete the block. Make 100 blocks.

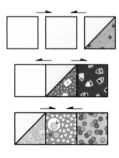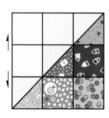

Make 100.

ASSEMBLING THE QUILT TOP

1. Lay out the blocks in 10 rows of 10 blocks each as shown in the quilt layout diagram, rotating them so that the light and dark halves of the blocks create the zigzag and diamond-shaped patterns.

2. Sew the blocks together in rows, pressing the seam allowances in opposite directions from one row to the next. Sew the rows together and press the seam allowances in one direction.

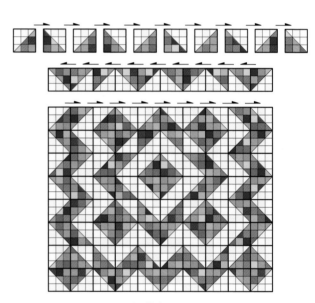

Quilt layout

3. Refer to "Borders with Butted Corners" on page 105 to measure, cut, and sew the 1½"-wide pink inner-border strips and the 4½"-wide green outer-border strips to the quilt top. Press all seam allowances toward the just-added strips.

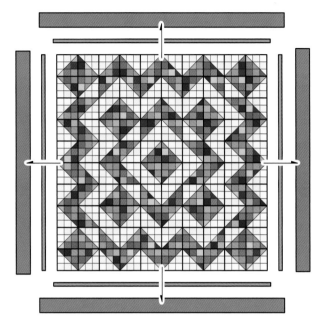

FINISHING THE QUILT

1. Layer the quilt top with backing and batting; baste.

2. Quilt as desired, or follow the quilting suggestion below.

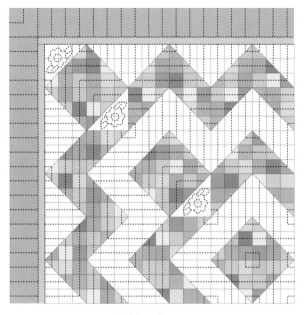

Quilting diagram

3. Referring to "Binding" on page 108, prepare the binding and sew it to the quilt. Add a label.

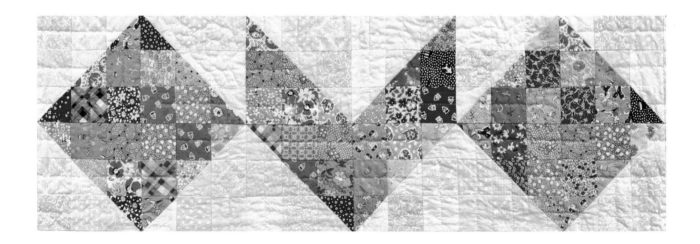

scrap nine patch

Finished quilt size: 68½" x 85½" ❊ Finished block size: 6" ❊ Number of blocks: 80

Setting traditional Nine Patch blocks on the diagonal gives a visually pleasing effect to the design. Varying the darks and lights in the blocks adds a whole new dimension to the quilt. Further varying the darks and lights in the alternating plain setting squares gives this quilt the illusion of having borders. Made with scraps, it becomes a real beauty. Mix in a few medium-light values with your light squares to add depth to the quilt.

MATERIALS

Yardage is based on 42"-wide fabric.

3⅝ yards *total* of assorted light prints for Nine Patch blocks and setting squares

1¾ yards *total* of assorted dark prints for Nine Patch blocks, setting squares, and setting triangles

1⅝ yards *total* of assorted medium prints for Nine Patch blocks

⅝ yard of dark print for binding

5⅝ yards of fabric for backing (2 widths pieced lengthwise)

74" x 91" piece of batting

CUTTING

Cut all strips across the width of fabric (selvage to selvage).

From the assorted dark prints, cut a total of:
11 strips, 2½" x 21"
5 squares, 6½" x 6½"
8 squares, 10½" x 10½"; cut each square twice diagonally to yield 32 setting triangles
2 squares, 6" x 6"; cut each square once diagonally to yield 4 corner triangles

From the assorted medium prints, cut a total of:
42 strips, 2½" x 21"

From the assorted light prints, cut a total of:
43 strips, 2½" x 21"
58 squares, 6½" x 6½"

From the dark print for binding, cut:
8 strips, 2¼" x 42"

By Sally Schneider, 1989, Puyallup, Washington.

MAKING THE BLOCKS

All of the Nine Patch blocks are made using just five different strip sets. After sewing each seam, press the seam allowances in the direction indicated by the arrows.

1. Sew the light print, medium print, and dark print strips together along their long edges as shown, paying close attention to value placement in each strip set. Make the number of strip sets shown for each color combination. Cut the strip sets into the number of 2½"-wide segments indicated, keeping the like segments together.

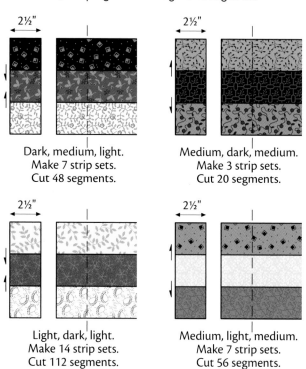

Dark, medium, light.
Make 7 strip sets.
Cut 48 segments.

Medium, dark, medium.
Make 3 strip sets.
Cut 20 segments.

Light, dark, light.
Make 14 strip sets.
Cut 112 segments.

Medium, light, medium.
Make 7 strip sets.
Cut 56 segments.

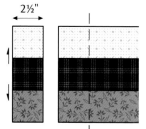

Light, dark, medium.
Make 1 strip set.
Cut 4 segments.

2. Sew together segments from each strip set as shown to make Nine Patch blocks. Make the number of blocks indicated for each color combination.

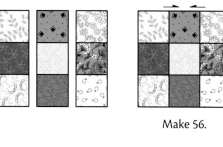

Make 56.

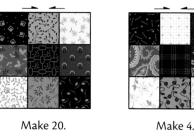

Make 20.   Make 4.

ASSEMBLING THE QUILT TOP

For detailed instructions, refer to "Quilts Set Diagonally" on page 103.

1. Lay out the Nine Patch blocks and 6½" light and dark setting squares in diagonal rows as shown in the quilt layout diagram. Pay close attention to the positioning of the Nine Patches and setting squares so that the values are placed to create the desired effect. Add the dark print side and corner setting triangles.

2. Sew the blocks, setting squares, and side triangles together in rows; press the seam allowances toward the setting squares and triangles.

3. Sew the rows together. Add the corner triangles last; press. The setting triangles were cut a bit oversized for easier cutting and piecing. Trim and square up the quilt top, making sure to leave ¼" beyond the points of all blocks for seam allowances.

Quilt layout

FINISHING THE QUILT

1. Layer the quilt with batting and backing; baste.

2. Quilt as desired, or follow the quilting suggestion at right.

3. Referring to "Binding" on page 108, prepare the binding and sew it to the quilt. Add a label.

Quilting diagram

spinning stars

Finished quilt size: 58½" x 70½" ✳ Finished block size: 12" ✳ Number of blocks: 20

Spinning Stars is a traditional pattern that I have adapted for scraps by using the fabric-menu technique on page 8. In Spinning Stars blocks, the two opposite-corner parallelograms are one color while the parallelograms in the other two corners are a different color. Although the fabrics vary from block to block, these colors and values remain the same throughout the quilt. The remaining parallelograms are always the same color within one block but differ in color from block to block. Finally, the triangles are always the same value.

MATERIALS

Yardage is based on 42"-wide fabric.

3¼ yards of light print for background

1 yard of dark blue print for outer border

⅞ yard of medium blue print for (A) stars

⅞ yard of dark blue print for (B) stars

¼ yard *each* of 20 assorted colors for (C) stars

⅜ yard of yellow print for inner border

⅝ yard of blue striped fabric for binding

3¾ yards of fabric for backing (2 widths pieced crosswise)

63" x 76" piece of batting

CUTTING

Cut all strips across the width of fabric (selvage to selvage).

From the light print, cut:
30 strips, 3½" x 42"; crosscut into 320 squares, 3½" x 3½"

From the medium blue print, cut:
4 strips, 6½" x 42"; crosscut into 40 rectangles, 3½" x 6½"
Label these rectangles A.

From the dark blue print for stars, cut:
4 strips, 6½" x 42"; crosscut into 40 rectangles, 3½" x 6½"
Label these rectangles B.

From *each* of the 20 assorted colors, cut:
1 strip, 6½" x 42"; crosscut into 4 rectangles, 3½" x 6½" (80 total)
Label these rectangles C.

From the yellow print for inner border, cut:
6 strips, 1½" x 42"

From the dark blue print for outer border, cut:
7 strips, 4½" x 42"

From the blue striped fabric, cut:
7 binding strips, 2¼" x 42"*

*When using a striped fabric as I did, you can cut it on the bias for a different look.

By Sally Schneider, 2008, Albuquerque, New Mexico.
Quilted by Leona VanLeeuwen.

MAKING THE BLOCKS

1. Referring to "Making Folded Corners" on page 100, sew a light print square to each end of each A, B, and C rectangle to create a parallelogram unit as shown. Make sure that both seams are angled in the same direction. Trim and press.

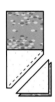

savvy bonus triangle squares

Rather than cutting off the unused triangles and tossing them away, you can make rectangles with a folded-corner plus a triangle-square unit while you're at it. Simply stitch another seam ½" from the first seam as shown. Cut between the sewn lines. Use this triangle-square unit for a border or for another quilt. See my website, www. sallyschneider.com, for more ideas for using these triangles.

2. Separate the units from step 1 into groups—one group of A units, one group of B units, and 20 groups of four matching C units.

3. For each block, lay out two A units, two B units, and four matching C units. Sew the A and C units together as shown. Then sew the B and C units together as shown. Press the seam allowances toward the C units. Make two of each.

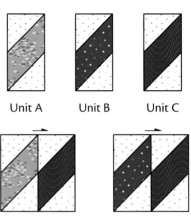

Unit A   Unit B   Unit C

Make 2.   Make 2.

savvy clipping

When sewing the units together, the seam allowances may twist when matching points. When this occurs, clip the seam allowance on the diagonal *almost* to the stitching line and press the two seam-allowance sections in opposite directions.

 ←Clip.

4. Join each color B/C unit to an A/C unit as shown, matching seam intersections. Press the seam allowances toward the A/C units.

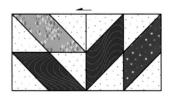

5. Sew the units together as shown, matching seam intersections carefully, and press. Make a total of 20 blocks.

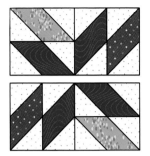 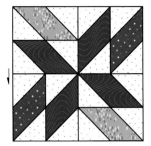

Make 20.

ASSEMBLING THE QUILT TOP

1. Lay out the blocks into five rows of four blocks each, rotating the blocks so that the A and B units form secondary light blue and dark blue stars as shown in the quilt layout diagram.

2. Sew the blocks together in rows, pressing the seam allowances in opposite directions from one row to the next. Then sew the rows together and press the seam allowances in one direction.

Quilt layout

3. Refer to "Borders with Butted Corners" on page 105 to measure, cut, and sew the 1½"-wide yellow inner-border strips, and then the 4½"-wide dark blue print outer-border strips to the quilt top. Press all seam allowances toward the just-added strips.

FINISHING THE QUILT

1. Layer the quilt with batting and backing; baste.

2. Quilt as desired.

3. Referring to "Binding" on page 108, prepare the binding and sew it to the quilt. Add a label.

thrifty nine patch

Finished quilt size: 67" x 82" ✷ Finished block size: 7½" ✷ Number of Thrifty blocks: 31
Number of Nine Patch blocks: 32

Derived from the time-honored Double Nine Patch pattern, the Thrifty Nine Patch design has an old-fashioned look. Four Patch corners set into a Nine Patch block is traditionally called the Thrift or Thrifty block. When you pair that block with alternating Nine Patch blocks, intersecting diagonal lines form and create a great deal of movement. It's a particularly good design for using a variety of fabrics in just two color families.

MATERIALS

Yardage is based on 42"-wide fabric.

2⅞ yards of light print for background*

1½ yards of dark blue print for outer border

1⅓ yards *total* of assorted blue prints for blocks

1 yard *total* of assorted red prints for blocks

1 yard of red print for inner border and binding

5¼ yards of fabric for backing (2 widths pieced lengthwise)

72" x 87" piece of batting

If you use a variety of light prints, you still need the total yardage indicated.

CUTTING

Cut all strips across the width of fabric (selvage to selvage).

From the light print, cut:
23 strips, 3" x 42"; crosscut into:
   36 strips, 3" x 21" (1 will be extra)
   62 squares, 3" x 3"
12 strips, 1¾" x 42"; cut each strip in half to yield 24 strips, 1¾" x 21" (1 will be extra)

From the assorted red prints, cut a total of:
6 strips, 3" x 21"
23 strips, 1¾" x 21"

From the assorted blue prints, cut a total of:
28 strips, 3" x 21"

From the red print, cut:
8 binding strips, 2¼" x 42"
7 border strips, 1½" x 42"

From the dark blue print, cut:
7 border strips, 6½" x 42"

By Sally Schneider, 1987, Honolulu, Hawaii.

MAKING THE THRIFTY BLOCKS

After sewing each seam, press the seam allowances in the direction indicated by the arrows.

1. Sew pairs of 1¾"-wide red strips and 1¾"-wide light print strips together along their long edges to make 23 strip sets. Cut the strip sets into 248 segments, 1¾" wide.

Make 23 strip sets.
Cut 248 segments.

2. Sew the segments from step 1 together in pairs to make a four-patch unit. Make a total of 124 four-patch units.

Make 124.

3. Sew a four-patch unit to each side of a light print 3" square, making sure the four-patch units are positioned as shown. Make 62 units.

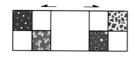

Make 62.

4. Sew two 3"-wide light print strips and one 3"-wide red strip together along their long edges to make six strip sets. Cut these strip sets into 31 segments, 3" wide.

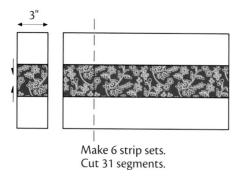

Make 6 strip sets.
Cut 31 segments.

5. Lay out two units from step 3 and one segment from step 4 as shown, making sure the dark squares in the four-patch units are positioned correctly. Sew the units together and press. Make a total of 31 Thrifty blocks.

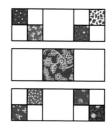

Make 31.

MAKING THE NINE PATCH BLOCKS

After sewing each seam, press the seam allowances in the direction indicated by the arrows.

1. Sew two 3"-wide blue strips and one 3"-wide light print strip together along their long edges to make 11 strip sets. Cut these strip sets into 64 segments, 3" wide.

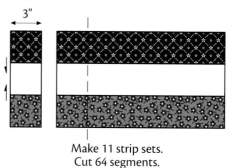

Make 11 strip sets.
Cut 64 segments.

2. Sew two 3"-wide light print strips and one 3"-wide blue strip together along their long edges to make six strip sets. Cut these strip sets into 32 segments, 3" wide.

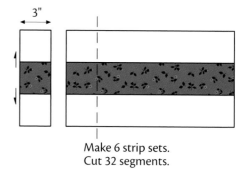

Make 6 strip sets.
Cut 32 segments.

3. Arrange the segments from steps 1 and 2 into Nine Patch blocks as shown. Sew the segments together and press. Make a total of 32 Nine Patch blocks.

 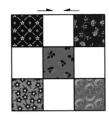

Make 32.

ASSEMBLING THE QUILT TOP

1. Lay out the Thrifty blocks and Nine Patch blocks in nine rows of seven blocks each. Start with a Nine Patch block in the outer corners and alternate with the Thrifty blocks. Sew the blocks together into rows, pressing the seam allowance toward the Nine Patch blocks.

2. Sew the rows together and press the seam allowances in one direction.

Quilt layout

3. Refer to "Borders with Butted Corners" on page 105 to measure, cut, and sew the 1½"-wide red inner-border strips, and then the 6½"-wide dark blue outer-border strips to the quilt top. Press all seam allowances toward the just-added strips.

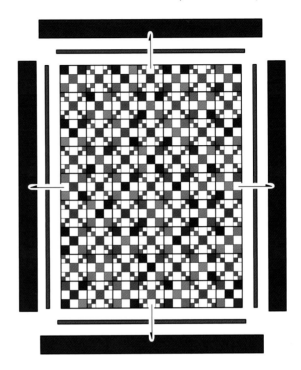

FINISHING THE QUILT

1. Layer the quilt with batting and backing; baste.

2. Quilt as desired.

3. Referring to "Binding" on page 108, prepare the binding and sew it to the quilt. Add a label.

wyoming valley star

Finished quilt size: 68½" x 86" ✳ Finished block size: 15" ✳ Number of blocks: 12

I grew up in Pennsylvania's Wyoming Valley, and making this quilt was a journey through my memories. Coordinated fabrics make up each Wyoming Valley Star block, but each block differs from the others within the quilt. The only fabric repeated throughout the quilt is the background.

MATERIALS

Yardage is based on 42"-wide fabric. Fat quarters measure 18" x 21" and fat eighths measure 9" x 21".

5 yards of light print for background, sashing, and border

1 fat quarter *each* of 12 assorted medium prints for Large Star blocks

1 fat eighth *each* of 12 assorted dark prints for Large Star blocks

1 fat eighth *each* of 12 assorted medium-light prints for Large Star blocks

40 assorted dark print squares, 3¾" x 3¾", for Small Star blocks (You'll need 2 matching squares of each print.)

20 assorted dark print squares, 3" x 3", for Small Star block centers

⅝ yard of bright blue fabric for binding

5½ yards of fabric for backing (2 widths pieced lengthwise)

74" x 91" piece of batting

CUTTING

Cut all strips across the width of fabric (selvage to selvage).

From the light print, cut:
2 strips, 15½" x 42"; crosscut into:

    14 strips, 3" x 15½"

    5 strips, 3" x 10½"

2 strips, 10½" x 42"; crosscut into 26 strips, 3" x 10½"

8 border strips, 4½" x 42"

4 strips, 3¾" x 42"; crosscut into 40 squares, 3¾" x 3¾"

20 strips, 3" x 42"; crosscut into:

    72 rectangles, 3" x 4"

    148 squares, 3" x 3" (reserve 4 squares for borders)

Continued on page 94.

By Sally Schneider, 1993, Puyallup, Washington.

Quilted by Kari Lane. From the collection of William George.

From *each* of the 12 assorted medium-light fat eighths, cut:

1 square, 5½" x 5½" (12 total)

2 strips, 3" x 14"; crosscut into 6 rectangles, 3" x 4" (72 total)

From *each* of the 12 assorted medium fat quarters, cut:

3 strips, 3" x 22"; crosscut into:

    8 rectangles, 3" x 5½" (96 total)

    4 squares, 3" x 3" (48 total)

From *each* of the 12 assorted dark fat eighths, cut:

8 squares, 3" x 3" (96 total)

From the bright blue for binding, cut:

8 strips, 2¼" x 42"

MAKING THE BLOCKS

Directions are for making one block. Each block is made from one medium-light print, one medium print, and one dark print. The same background fabric is used for all of the blocks. For each block select the following: one medium-light print square with six matching rectangles, eight matching medium print rectangles with four matching squares, and eight matching dark print squares. Repeat to make a total of 12 blocks. After sewing each seam, press the seam allowances in the direction indicated by the arrows.

1. Referring to "Method One" on page 99, layer a 3" x 4" light print rectangle and a medium-light rectangle right sides together and draw 45° lines from opposite corners on the wrong side of the light rectangle. Sew on both drawn lines, and then cut the rectangles apart between the lines. Press the seam allowances toward the darker fabric. Make 12 matching triangle squares.

Make 12 matching
triangle squares.

2. Referring to "Making Folded Corners" on page 100, place a 3" light print square on one end of a medium print rectangle. Make a total of eight matching units; sew four with seams facing in one direction and four with seams in the opposite direction. Trim and press.

Make 4.   Make 4.

3. In the same manner, sew a matching 3" dark print square to the opposite end of each rectangle. Be sure to stitch the seams in the same direction as the light print squares.

Make 4.   Make 4.

4. Sew two units from step 3 together as shown, pressing the seam allowance open. Make four side units.

Make 4.

5. For the center unit, use the folded-corner technique to place medium print squares on opposite corners of a medium-light square. Stitch, trim, and press. Repeat with the remaining two corners.

Make 1.

6. For each corner unit, lay out three triangle squares and one 3" light print square in a four-patch arrangement as shown. Sew the pieces together in pairs, and then sew the pairs together to complete the unit. Make four corner units.

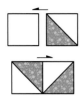

Make 4.

7. Lay out one center unit, four side units, and four corner units in a nine-patch arrangement as shown. Sew the units together in rows, and then sew rows together to complete a Wyoming Valley Star block. Make a total of 12 blocks.

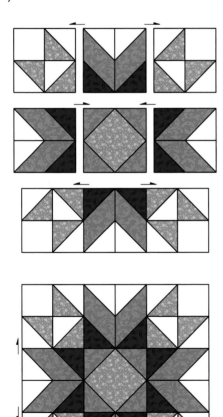

Make 12.

ASSEMBLING THE QUILT TOP

1. Referring to "Method Two" on page 100, place 3¾" light print and dark print squares right sides together, and then draw a diagonal line from corner to corner on the wrong side of each light square. Sew ¼" from each side of the marked line. Cut the squares apart on the line to create two triangle squares. Press the seam allowances toward the dark triangle.

Make 80.

2. Place two matching triangle squares right sides together. Draw a diagonal line on the wrong side of one square, crossing the seam. Stitch ¼" from each side of the marked line. Cut the squares apart on the line to create two quarter-square-triangle units. Press. Make a total of 80 quarter-square-triangle units.

Make 80.

3. Referring to the quilt layout diagram on page 96, lay out the blocks and the 10½"-long light print sashing strips in four rows of three blocks each, beginning and ending each row with a sashing strip. Position the remaining 10½"-long sashing strips between the blocks rows and at the top and bottom of the first and last block rows. Place the 15½"-long background sashing strips around the outside edges as shown. Then add the 20 dark print squares and the quarter-square-triangle units, making sure to use four matching quarter-square-triangle units for each small star.

4. Working with one sashing strip at a time, sew a quarter-square-triangle unit to each end of a 10½"-long sashing strip. After pressing, make sure to return the unit to its correct position in the quilt layout so that the small stars will have like-colored star points.

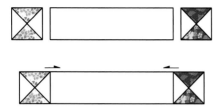

5. Carefully examine the layout to make sure that each piece is positioned correctly, referring to the layout diagram as needed. Once you are satisfied, sew the pieces together into rows and press. Sew the rows together and press. Refer to "Quilts with Sashing Strips" on page 104 for details as needed.

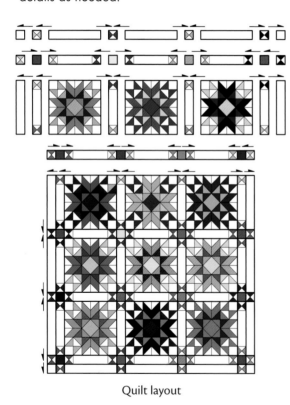

Quilt layout

6. Refer to "Borders with Butted Corners" on page 105 to measure, cut, and sew the 4½"-wide light print outer-border strips to the quilt top. Press all seam allowances toward the outer-border strips.

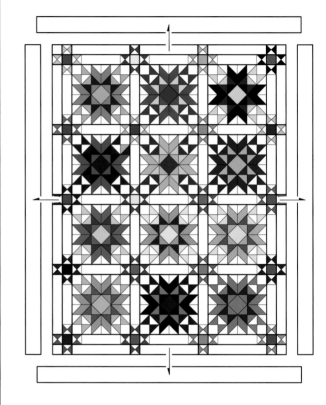

FINISHING THE QUILT

1. Layer the quilt with batting and backing; baste.

2. Quilt as desired.

3. Referring to "Binding" on page 108, prepare the binding and sew it to the quilt. Add a label.

quiltmaking basics

All my quilts are made with just a few basic techniques—techniques that should be in the repertoire of any confident beginning quilter. None of them are difficult, but sometimes the way I combine the techniques makes a quilt look more complicated than it really is. I don't do hard—I do easy that sometimes looks hard! In this section of the book I'll describe these techniques, along with some other ones that you need to know to finish up your quilt.

SEWING ACCURATE SEAM ALLOWANCES

The most important skill for a quilter to master is making an accurate ¼"-wide seam allowance. We all think we can sew a ¼" seam, but it's not as easy as it appears. You only have to be off a little to make a big difference in the way your pieces fit together. Even when I used my ¼" presser foot and the ¼" guide line engraved on my sewing machine, my pieces still turned out too small. I had to find where my own personal ¼" guide was on my machine.

Do the following test to make sure your seam allowances are accurate. Cut three strips, each 2" x 6". Sew them together using your personal ¼"-wide seam allowance, and then press the seams to one side. Measure the strip set. It should be exactly 5" wide. If it's more or less than 5", even by just a little bit, your ¼" seam allowance is not correct.

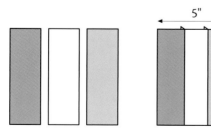

Repeat the sewing test, adjusting the seam allowance until you get it correct. When you do, take a file card or a small rectangle of template plastic and, with the sewing machine needle unthreaded, place the edge of the file card on your perfect ¼" mark. Stitch a line onto the file card or plastic. Now you have a record of your perfect ¼" on file, and you can always find it again. You can even change sewing machines and keep an accurate seam allowance. Just line up the stitched line with the machine's needle. The edge of the card is your perfect ¼" mark. I stick a piece of moleskin, or a piece of masking tape, on my machine to use as a stitching guide.

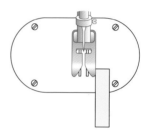

ROTARY CUTTING

Instructions for quick-and-easy rotary cutting are provided wherever possible. All measurements include standard ¼"-wide seam allowances. If you are unfamiliar with rotary cutting, read the brief introduction that follows.

1. Fold the fabric and match selvages, aligning the crosswise and lengthwise grains as much as possible. Place the folded edge closest to you on the cutting mat. Align a square ruler along the folded edge of the fabric. Place a long, straight ruler to the left of the square ruler, just covering the uneven raw edges on the left side of the fabric.

2. Remove the square ruler and cut along the right edge of the long ruler, rolling the rotary cutter away from you. Discard this strip. (Reverse this procedure if you are left-handed.)

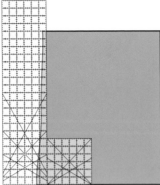

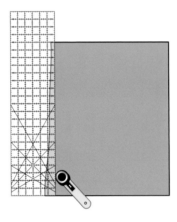

3. To cut strips, align the newly cut edge of the fabric with the ruler markings at the required width. For example, to cut a 3"-wide strip, place the 3" ruler mark on the edge of the fabric.

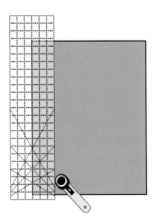

4. To cut squares and rectangles, cut strips in the required widths. Trim the selvage ends of the strips. Align the left edge of the strips with the correct ruler markings. Cut the strips into squares or rectangles. Continue cutting until you have the required number of pieces.

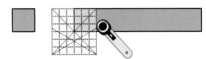

MAKING STRIP SETS

You can assemble blocks or parts of blocks made with just squares and rectangles by cutting strips of fabric, sewing them together in a specific order to make a strip set, and then cutting the strip sets into segments. You'll use this method to make quilts like "Scrap Nine Patch" (page 80), "Thrifty Nine Patch" (page 88), "Burgoyne Surrounded" (page 30), and "For My Dad" (page 48).

1. With right sides together, sew strips together along the long edges in the order required for your design. Press the seams toward the darker fabric. Use steam, but press carefully to avoid stretching. Press from the right side first, then turn the unit over and press from the wrong side to be sure that all the seam allowances face in the proper direction.

2. Align a horizontal line on a small ruler with a seam line and place a longer ruler to the left so that the end of the strip set is covered. Remove the small ruler and make a rotary cut along the right edge of the longer ruler to trim the

uneven edge of the strip set. Cut the strip set into segments using the width specified in the directions for your quilt.

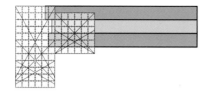

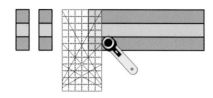

3. Join the segments to make the blocks or units required for your quilt.

MAKING TRIANGLE SQUARES

My method for making these units has evolved over the years as I learn or think of new ways to make half-square-triangle units called triangle squares. I now use two main methods, both of which I will describe here. All the directions in the book use one of these two methods.

method one

1. Cut two rectangles (one light and one dark, or whatever is required for your quilt). The size of the shorter side of the rectangle is determined by the *unfinished*, or cut, size of the triangle square. The longer side is 1" longer than the short side. For example, if your quilt required 2" finished triangle squares, the cut size is 2½" (2" plus ½" for seam allowance). Therefore your rectangle would be 2½" x 3½".

2. Layer light print and dark print rectangles right sides together. On the wrong side of the lighter rectangle, draw two 45° lines from opposite corners. You can use a bias square ruler, or I have a tool called "The Gizmo" that you can also use to determine both lines at the same

time. To draw the lines using a bias square ruler, align the 45° line on the square ruler with either the side or the bottom of the rectangle, making sure the edge of the ruler goes through the corner of the rectangle.

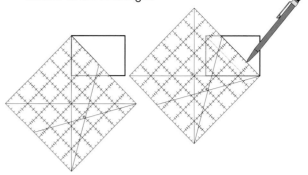

To use the Gizmo, line up the tool with a corner of the rectangle as shown below. Draw a line along both sides of the Gizmo—the lines should go from the top left to the bottom right corner and should be at a 45° angle.

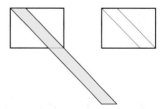

3. Sew on each of the lines you drew, and then cut between the lines with a rotary cutter or scissors to make two triangle squares. Press the seam allowances toward the darker fabric, and then trim the dog-ears from the corners. With this method the seam allowance will be slightly

wider than ¼"; if you prefer to have exact ¼"
seams, you can trim the seam allowances to the
correct size.

method two

1. Cut two squares ⅞" larger than the desired
   finished size of the triangle square. For example,
   if the finished triangle square is 2", you'll cut
   2⅞" squares. Place the squares right sides
   together, and then draw a diagonal line from
   one corner to the opposite corner on the lighter
   or easier to see square.

2. Sew ¼" from each side of the diagonal line.
   Cut the squares apart on the drawn line, and
   then press the seam allowances of the resulting
   triangle squares toward the darker fabric. Trim
   the dog-ears from the corners.

Stitch.   Cut.   Press.
                             Trim corners.

savvy chain stitching

Prepare assorted pieces using either
method before you start a new project.
Then, instead of using scraps to start and
end your chain stitching, sew the seams
of these pieces. You'll quickly have lots
of triangle squares for a new project!

MAKING FOLDED CORNERS

I love this method for adding a triangle to the tip of
a square or a rectangle, or for making flying-geese
units and parallelograms. You need only squares
and rectangles. The measuring is simple, as is the
sewing. You don't even need to draw a sewing line.
Although there is a little more fabric waste, the time
and energy saved make it well worth it.

1. Place a piece of blue masking tape on your
   machine. I prefer blue tape because it shows
   up better on the machine. You can also use a
   ruler and just draw a line with a permanent
   pen such as a Sharpie marker. The right edge
   of the tape should be in a straight line from the
   needle toward you. Allow the tape to extend as
   far toward you as possible. If your machine is
   portable and you don't have a wide bed, attach
   the end of the tape to the table your machine
   sits on. Trim the tape away from the feed dogs.

2. Place a small square on one corner of a larger
   square (or rectangle), right sides together and
   raw edges aligned. Begin sewing exactly in the
   corner of the top square. As you stitch, keep
   the opposite corner directly on the edge of the
   masking tape.

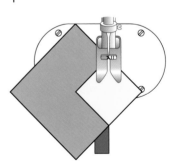

3. Trim away the excess fabric, leaving a ¼" seam allowance; then press the resulting triangle toward the corner.

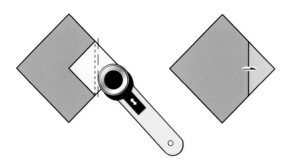

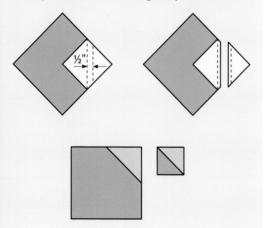

savvy bonus triangle squares

If the smaller square is 3½" or larger, stitch a second seam ½" from the first seam as shown, and then cut between the two stitching lines. You have the square with the folded corner, plus a bonus triangle square that you can use for another project. See my website, www.sallyschneider.com, for ideas for using these bonus triangle-square units.

MAKING MARY'S TRIANGLE UNITS

This is a little trick I developed years ago to quickly make Shaded Four Patch block units. It is named for my friend, Mary Kelleher, who was sitting next to me on the ski lift when I got the original idea. Use these units to make "Askew" on page 12 and "MT Triangled" on page 68. For each pair of finished units, you need to start with two triangle squares or plain squares, two small rectangles, and one large rectangle.

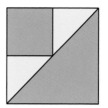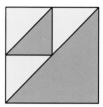

Mary's Triangle units
with squares and with triangles

1. Make triangle squares or cut plain squares the required size.

2. Cut two rectangles that are 1" longer than the triangle square (or plain square). If the square is 2" x 2", cut the rectangles 2" x 3".

3. Using an accurate ¼"-wide seam allowance, sew the triangle squares (or plain squares) to the rectangles as shown.

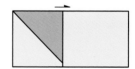

Make 2.

4. Sew the pair of units from step 3 together as shown. Be sure to match the outside edges.

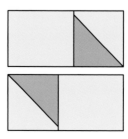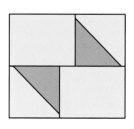

5. In the center of the unit, clip the seam allowance through the seam line as shown. From the wrong side, press the seam allowances toward the rectangles. There will be a small hole in the unit where you clipped, but you will eventually be cutting through this hole and it will not appear in your finished block.

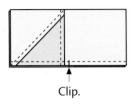

Clip.

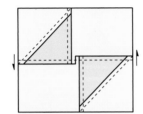

Press seams away
from triangles.

6. Cut a square of template material equal to the short edge of the rectangle made in step 5. Cut the square in half diagonally. If the rectangle is 4" x 5", cut the square 4" x 4". You can also use the Magic Triangle ruler, following the directions included with the ruler.

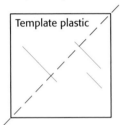
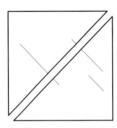

Template plastic

7. To mark the sewing line, place the template on the wrong side of the pieced rectangle, with the corner of the template on the triangle square (or plain square). Draw the diagonal line across the pieced rectangle unit as shown. Place the

template on the opposite corner, again with the template's corner on the triangle square. Mark a second sewing line.

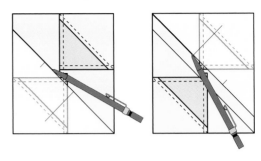

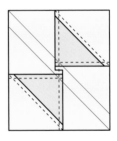

Mark stitching lines.

8. Place a large rectangle of another fabric, right sides together, with the pieced rectangle. Sew on each of the lines you drew, and then cut between them. Press the seam allowances toward the large triangles. You will have two units as shown.

The seam allowances will be greater than ¼". If you prefer to have exact ¼" seams, you can trim them to the correct size.

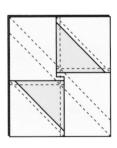
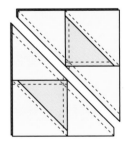

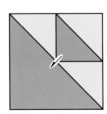
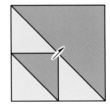

Makes 2.

assembling
and finishing the quilt

Many people like to square up their blocks before arranging them and sewing them together. I prefer not to do that because I'm afraid that I will cut off points that need to match other points. I much prefer to pin matching points together so that I know they'll come out properly.

QUILTS WITH STRAIGHT SETS

In this traditional setting, blocks are set side by side in horizontal or vertical rows. The blocks will be parallel to the sides of the quilt.

1. On a design wall or other place where you can see all of the blocks, lay out the blocks in rows as shown in the quilt layout for your project. Make sure the colors are well distributed and that the blocks are rotated correctly.

2. Sew the blocks together in horizontal rows. Press the seam allowances in opposite directions from one row to the next.

3. Sew the rows together, being careful to match the seams from row to row. Press the seam allowances in one direction.

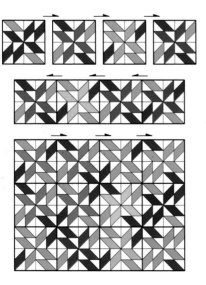

QUILTS SET DIAGONALLY

In a diagonally set quilt, the blocks are set on point and arranged in diagonal rows. The blocks will be at a 45° angle to the sides of the quilt. The spaces along the edge of a diagonally set quilt are filled with side and corner setting triangles. These triangles are cut so that the outside edge of the triangle is on the straight grain of the fabric to ensure that the edges don't stretch when you attach the border.

Side setting triangles   Corner triangles

The directions for each quilt tells you how large to cut the triangles. The triangles are intentionally cut larger than necessary and trimmed after the quilt top is complete. Lay out the blocks, side setting triangles, and corner setting triangles as shown in the quilt layout diagram for your project. Sew the pieces together in diagonal rows. Sew the rows together, matching the seams from row to row. Press as directed in the project instructions.

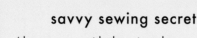

Notice that the right-angle corners of the triangles match the block edges and the sharper points of the triangles extend beyond the edge of the block. After the triangles are stitched, lay your ruler across the top of the block, keeping the edge of the ruler even with the raw edge of the block. Trim the triangles even with the raw edge.

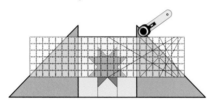

Once the quilt top is complete, you'll need to square up the edges of the quilt. Align the ¼" mark on your ruler with the outermost points of the blocks. Use a rotary cutter to trim the excess fabric, leaving a ¼"-wide seam allowance. Square the corners of the quilt as necessary.

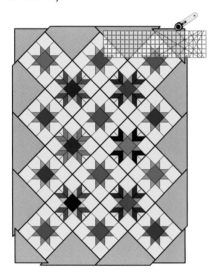

QUILTS WITH SASHING STRIPS

Many of the quilts in this book are assembled with sashing strips between the blocks. Some of them have pieced sashing strips that form stars when the strips are put together. All the quilts with sashing strips have corner squares, or cornerstones, where the strips meet.

1. On a design wall or other place where you can see the entire quilt, lay out the blocks, sashing strips, and corner squares in rows as shown in the quilt layout for your project. If the sashing strips have pieced units on the ends, arrange these to your liking and assemble the sashing strips if necessary. To make sure the sashing strips stay in order, sew them one at a time, and then return the strip to its place in the quilt layout.

2. Once the sashing strips are assembled and arranged to your liking, pick up the top row of sashing strips and corner squares. Sew them together in order and press the seam allowances toward the sashing strips. Return the row to its original position.

   If your quilt has pieced sashing strips, you will have two rows of sashing at the top and at the bottom of the quilt; these are required to complete the patterns in the sashing strips.

3. Pick up the next row of blocks and sashing strips and sew them together in order. Press the seam allowances toward the sashing strips. Return this row to its proper position.

4. Continue sewing rows of sashing strips/corner squares and rows of sashing strips/blocks until they are all complete. Then sew the rows together in the proper order to complete the quilt top. Press the seam allowances toward the sashing strips/corner squares rows.

BORDERS WITH BUTTED CORNERS

I prefer to cut border strips across the width of the fabric and join them end to end as needed. Less fabric is required when borders are cut this way. To keep your quilt square, it is essential to always measure through the center of the quilt and cut the border strips to fit precisely before sewing them to the quilt top. I find it easier to measure using the actual border strip rather than a ruler.

1. To measure borders, lay two strips across the center of the quilt lengthwise. Trim both ends even with the raw edge of the quilt. Fold each border strip in quarters, lightly crease the folds, and mark the creases with a pin. In the same manner, mark the same positions on the sides of the quilt top.

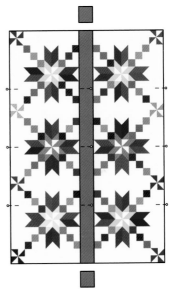

2. Pin the borders to the quilt top, matching the pin markings and ends. Pin about every 3" along the border, easing if necessary. Sew the side

borders to the quilt with a ¼"-wide seam allowance and press the seam allowance toward the border strips.

3. Repeat this procedure for the top and bottom borders.

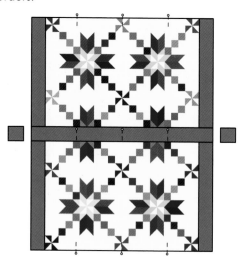

QUILT BACKS

I find that running the seam lengthwise on a pieced backing often requires more fabric than is necessary. Instead, I prefer to calculate the yardage required for quilt backs to allow the least amount of excess fabric. When piecing the backing, be sure to trim off the selvages before sewing the pieces together and press the seam allowances open to reduce the bulk.

For all quilts up to 75" long, I piece the backing with one crosswise seam in the center. Measure the width of the quilt, add 6", and then double this measurement. Divide the result by 36" and that equals the number of yards of fabric you need to purchase.

For quilts that are longer than 75" and up to 75" wide, I piece the backing with one lengthwise seam in the center. Measure the length of the quilt, add 6", and then double this measurement. Divide the result by 36" and that equals the number of yards of fabric you'll need.

I piece backings for quilts even larger than this with three lengths of fabric. Measure the shortest side of the quilt, add 6", triple this measurement, and divide the result by 36" to calculate the number of yards of fabric you'll need.

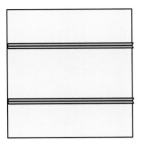

After the backing is pieced, press it to remove all wrinkles and fold lines, and to make sure all the seams are flat.

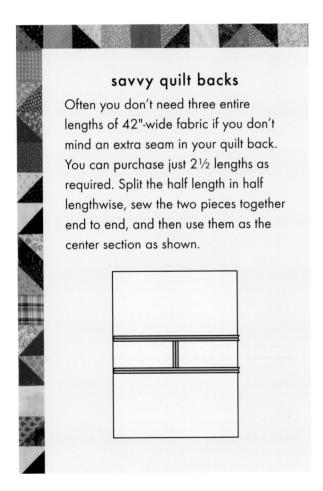

savvy quilt backs

Often you don't need three entire lengths of 42"-wide fabric if you don't mind an extra seam in your quilt back. You can purchase just 2½ lengths as required. Split the half length in half lengthwise, sew the two pieces together end to end, and then use them as the center section as shown.

BASTING

Baste your quilt on a flat, clean surface such as a large dining room table or several banquet tables pushed together. Sometimes you can use the tables at a quilt shop when they are not holding classes. Unfold your batting the day before you plan to baste the quilt to let it rest, or place it in the dryer on air dry for about 20 minutes to remove some of the wrinkles.

1. Spread the backing, wrong side up, on the table and anchor it with masking tape or binder clips. Be careful not to stretch the backing out of shape.

2. Spread the batting over the backing, smoothing out any wrinkles. Center the pressed quilt top, right side up, on top of the batting. Smooth out any wrinkles and make sure the quilt-top edges are parallel to the edges of the batting.

3. For hand quilting, baste with needle and thread, starting in the center and working diagonally to each corner. Then baste a grid of horizontal and vertical lines about 6" apart. Finish by basting around the edges about ⅛" from the quilt-top edge.

4. For machine quilting, baste the layers with No. 2 rustproof safety pins. Place pins about 3" to 4" apart; try to avoid areas where you intend to quilt. Finish by machine basting around the edges about ⅛" from the quilt-top edge.

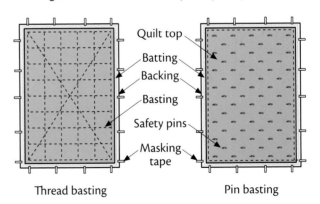

Thread basting   Pin basting

BINDING

For a double-fold binding, I cut straight-grain strips 2¼" wide across the full width of the fabric. You will need enough strips to go around the perimeter of the quilt plus 10" for making seams and turning corners.

1. Sew the binding strips together to make one long strip. Join the strips at right angles, right sides together, and stitch across the corner as shown. Trim the excess fabric, leaving a ¼"-wide seam, and press the seam allowances open.

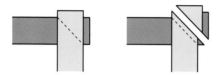

2. Fold the strip in half lengthwise, wrong sides together, and press.

3. Trim the excess backing and batting even with the quilt top. Starting about 15" from a corner, align the raw edge of the binding with the raw edges of the quilt top. Leaving about a 6" tail of binding and using a walking foot and a ⅜"-wide seam allowance, start sewing the binding strip to the quilt. Stop ⅜" from the first corner; backstitch and remove the quilt from the machine.

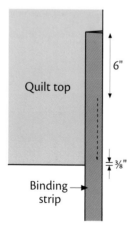

4. To miter the corner, fold the binding up and away from the quilt so the fold forms a 45° angle, and then fold it back down on itself, even with the edge you will now be sewing. The fold should be aligned with the corner of the quilt top.

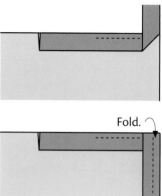

Fold.

5. Beginning ⅜" from the corner and backstitching to secure the stitches, sew the binding to the next side of the quilt in the same fashion, stopping ⅜" from the next corner. Repeat the process, mitering each corner as you come to it. On the last side of the quilt, stop stitching about 10" from the point where you started attaching the binding and backstitch. Remove the quilt from the machine.

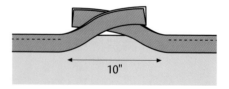

10"

6. Fold one end of the binding back on itself. Fold the other end of the binding back on itself. Butt the folded ends together and press the fold.

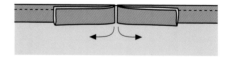

7. Unfold the two ends of the binding and overlap the ends, matching the center of the pressed Xs. The right end should be on top of the left end, right sides together, as shown. Draw the seam line diagonally between the points where the strips intersect. Pin and sew the binding ends together on the drawn line. Trim the excess fabric, leaving a ¼" seam allowance, and press the seam open.

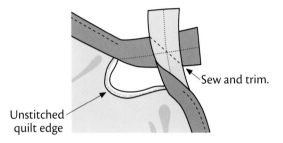

Unstitched quilt edge

Sew and trim.

8. Refold the binding, align the edges with the raw edges of the quilt top, and sew it in place.

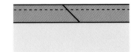

Complete stitching.

9. Fold the binding to the back of the quilt so that it covers the machine stitching. Hand stitch in place, folding the miters as you reach each corner.

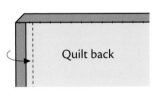

Quilt back

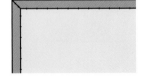

LABELS

Always add a label to your quilt. Years from now, your family will want to know who made the quilt and when it was made. The label should include at least your name, your town, and the year the quilt was made.

You can write the information on a piece of muslin with a permanent marker and stitch it to the quilt, or you can make a fancier label using other needlework techniques or colored markers. There are even labels available to purchase as fabric yardage. If your sewing machine does lettering, you can make a label that way.

Stitch the label to the back of the quilt.